THE BUSINESS OF HEALTH

Non-clinical Skills to Build Your Practice

Ross Tomkins

AHG

First published in Great Britain 2019 by Purple Star Design.

Published and book design by Clare McCabe
www.purplestarpublishing.co.uk

ISBN-13: 978-1-5272-3793-3

DISCLAIMER
The contents of this book do not constitute advice and is not intended as a substitute for professional business advice.
This book is published in good faith but neither the publisher or the author shall be held liable for any alleged damage arising from any suggestion or information contained in this book.

I wouldn't have written this without the unswerving support of my wife, Joanne.
You are my rock, my foundations and give me the strength to pursue my dreams.
Thank you

CONTENTS

PRAISE FOR THE BUSINESS OF HEALTH

Whether you're a recent graduate, mid-career therapist or owner of a growing practice, I firmly believe that we should all be spending an equal amount of time improving our non-clinical skills as our clinical skills. For every hour of clinical research on diagnosis and manual techniques, an equal amount of time should be spent on improving your listening, communicating and time management skills. I sometimes wish that I'd had a mentor share with me the importance of non-clinical skills much earlier in my career. It would have speeded up my learning from the very start. Fortunately, Ross' book is here now not only to teach the importance of non-clinical skills, but, with 19 chapters of content to help you become the best practice owner and well-rounded healthcare professional you can be.

Tristan White, The Physio Co. and author of Culture Is Everything

Therapists just want to help people, but until now they had to try to grow their business through trial and error. The Business of Health is literally packed full of tips to help Healthcare businesses to provide incredible service as well as the lifestyle that so many business owners crave. The first time you read this book, you can put some of the advice into immediate action and get some instant wins, but I urge you to keep re-reading it and keep using it as it will help you develop and progress in business and reach your personal goals. Brilliant!

Andrew Byrne MCSP, HCPC. Director, www.truephysio.co.uk

In writing The Business of Health: Non Clinical Skills to Build Your Practice, Tomkins has created a work that is close to my heart. His central argument is that it is the non-medical skills that are essential in a therapy business, and I agree. The Business of Health covers not only the sometimes-called 'soft skills' of listening, rapport-building and body language but also the more traditional topics of marketing and technology. The four key tenets underpinning the book are 1. respect everyone, 2. be memorable, 3. be positive and 4. Be the best. You can't argue with those as qualities to which we might all aspire. Each chapter is easy to digest, with top tips and short paragraphs for key information. What I like about this book is that Tomkins is not afraid to share his experiences, including some of the mistakes he's made. A physiotherapist at heart he does not shy away from the need to measure performance and in Chapter 5: Hiring for Attitude, he tackles some of the difficulties we all face in making assessments. For example, by asking questions such as, 'how do you assess what a person's core values are?' Importantly, this is not just a book filled with anecdotes, it teaches you something. With many years experience Tomkins has established and nurtured a leading healthcare company, Therapy Direct. We've all met people who say one thing but do another. Having worked for Therapy Direct it's reassuring to know that Tomkins lives by his word. There is important information in this book that anyone running, developing or thinking about starting a therapy business ought to know. It's a book I wish I'd written myself.

Jane Johnson. Senior Physiotherapist and Author of Postural Assessment

Practitioners or practice managers, either just starting out on their journey in Healthcare or even well-established will be certain to gain valuable insight into how to expand their business from this book. It's filled with a number of good tips on; how to build rapport, leveraging and emotional intelligence, from an author who has valuable experience in the sector, developing from a sole practitioner to running a well-respected company within work focused Physiotherapy and rehabilitation. The books use of mild humour, true life experiences and famous quotes really does add a nice depth of thought. One of many valuable parts of this book I shall take away is the importance of leveraging and effective use of time and resource. The quote 'TIME is the most valuable resource in the entire universe. If you lose your MONEY, you can always make more; if you lose you TIME though its gone forever', will influence my thought process for many years to come!

Chris Bartlett BSc (Hons), GSR, MSc. Head of Technical Development, Overland Health

INTRODUCTION

"If you think you can do a thing or think you can't do a thing, you're right." **- Henry Ford**

Doubt and fear clawed at the edges of my mind whilst I wrestled with the idea of writing this book.

I don't have a PhD, I haven't completed a Master's degree and I'm no modern-day, physiotherapeutic guru. There are others out there in the big wide world who are probably far more qualified than I to write a book on the subject ... not that I've seen any like the one I knew I wanted to write. Month after month, I scanned new Amazon titles to see if someone had published something similar, expecting a book cover with its grinning author to pop up on my screen at any moment.

It never did.

The urge to put down in writing what I've learned over the years and now share with others grew. At the same time, that nagging little voice would try to put me down.

"What if nobody reads any of it save the above quote from Henry Ford?" it would pipe up, smothering any feelings of excitement and creativity I had.

Eventually, I grew tired of the yo-yoing, 'should I, shouldn't I' inner squabbling – as did my family. Who knew if anyone would read a

book that I've written? So what? One thing was for sure: nobody would ever read a book that I haven't written.
And, truth be told, I am absolutely qualified to write it.

I have almost 20 years' of industry experience – thirteen years as a business owner who now employs thirty-six, full-time staff and four part-time subcontractors. I have useful insight to offer business owners: how to avoid some of my past pitfalls and work fewer hours by being smarter. How they can spend more time with their families and friends – doing the things they love. I learned the value of the lesson "Do what you love" in a round about way.

As a sporty kid in the Eighties, I found my niche in football and tennis, spending as much time as I could outside of our dysfunctional family home. Things were stressful at home – there was a lack of balanced support and often we went without basic necessities, such as hot water. My sport was a kind of safe place – a supportive environment where I could really feel that I was achieving something.

I was good at both tennis and football, and as time went on I developed my skills and planned a future in coaching – something that would enable me to continue to exercise my strengths.

Fate had other plans, however. I developed 'Anterior Knee Pain' – although nobody could diagnose exactly what was causing it for a long time. After several months and numerous physiotherapy appointments, my therapist advised me against a career in sport. Naturally, I was very disappointed ... but as a sporty kid who was fascinated by how the body works during sport, I soon discovered a new goal: I decided to study to become a physiotherapist.

A short while into my university studies, I had a Eureka moment. The pain that had put paid to my coaching career before it had even started was nothing to do with my knee. As it turned out, I had a leg-length imbalance (quite an obvious one, at that) which was likely to be the underlying cause of my old knee pain.

Why hadn't all of those physiotherapists noticed that? I hadn't even graduated yet, and it was quite clear to me already.
I can't say that I wasn't upset at first. After all, I'd had my heart set on a coaching career – had spent my entire childhood training for it and loving my sport, only to have it unnecessarily ruled out by what I considered to be poor professionals. But as my studies continued, I fell in love with physiotherapy and those old, hard-done-by feelings began to fade. Ironically, as my career has progressed and I have gained experience, I doubt my leg length discrepancy was the cause but that could be the basis of another book.

Regardless of the reason, I had stumbled painfully into a new dream. I loved physiotherapy and by now couldn't imagine a future doing anything else. If my knee pain had been properly diagnosed earlier, I wouldn't have discovered this amazing, new life.

Inadvertently, I had learned my first valuable lesson in business:

DO WHAT YOU LOVE.
This book is presented in four Parts – each focusing on a core value of my business:

PART 1: RESPECT EVERYONE
PART 2: BE MEMORABLE
PART 3: BE POSITIVE
PART 4: BE THE BEST

Each of these core values is of vital importance to me as each teaches us valuable lessons. They provide the foundation for the information and subject matter within these pages.

The most successful physiotherapists are not necessarily the ones with the most letters after their name: they are the ones who are better at business.

To run a successful healthcare business you need the skills in the following areas:

- Medical expertise
- Soft skills (listening, communication, etc.)
- Administration and Customer Service
- Finances (credit control)
- Marketing (social media and networking)
- Mindset

As there is an abundance of books, courses and educators teaching everything from acupuncture to Zumba for physiotherapy, I don't want to focus on these. I would like to open you up to the possibility that non-medical skills are essential for success in every business. To that end, this book focuses on the softer skills and mindset required for you to realise your goals.

For more information on the central business services of Administration, Customer Service, Finance and Marketing, please visit our website www.the-ahg.com and Facebook group www.facebook.com and search: 'Advanced Health Group'.

My intention for the book and hope for you is that it may provide a useful blueprint for many of the skills you'll need to nurture in order to build your own healthcare business. If you're on the starting blocks, I hope that it may give you the affirmation you need to start and grow your new enterprise. After all, the grass isn't 'always greener on the other side': it's greener where you water it.

Love what you do and practice growth!
Ross Tomkins

PART 1
RESPECT EVERYONE

CHAPTER 1: LISTENING

"One of the most sincere forms of respect is actually listening to what another has to say". **- Bryant H. McGill**

Of all the skills you need to start and grow a successful healthcare business – indeed, any business – this is it.

I place so much importance on 'listening', in fact, that I'd say it was the catalyst and bedrock for my own business, "Therapy Direct Healthcare".

ACTIVE LISTENING

Let me be clear: when I use the term 'listening' here and elsewhere in this book, I am talking about 'Active Listening'. This is a term used for the concentrated art of hearing more than that which is being said in any conversation, be it verbal, non-verbal or written. There is so much more to Active Listening than simply understanding the text and context of what somebody is trying to communicate. It involves your studying the subtext of the conversation too – reading between the lines of what is being said and reaching to the very heart of the matter.

Active Listening in this way is one of the most useful skills that anyone can develop. In everyday life, most people are not so much listening as simply waiting for a pause in the other person's talking to get their comment in.

In contrast, Active Listening allows the listener to respond to the other person with pertinent questions and so to gain more useful information. As a result, the Active Listener is in the best position to build stronger relationships with others.

One of its defining characteristics is liberal use of pause. Most people in Western society fill what they perceive to be 'holes' in conversation flow with more words, never allowing a simple pause to follow a statement. Pause is a useful tool in any conversation; it can impress upon someone the real meaning and true intention behind the sentence that preceded it. Ironically, far more can be communicated with a pause than in a stream of words.

Take note when you are out today – at work, while you're shopping, listening to the radio in your car – and see who is really listening and who is simply waiting to speak.

My own epiphany in Active Listening was a drawn out one ... far from my being hit by a blinding moment of realisation, it dawned on me over several months that my patients' progress had more to do with the two thirds of their lives that I knew virtually nothing about.

I knew about their physical state when they came to see me but that was all. If I were to be able to diagnose and recommend powerful treatment for them that would definitely work, I needed to know more about their working lives. That's where they spent the majority of their time, after all.

It is common knowledge that we should warm up our bodies properly before starting an occasional, forty-minute exercise routine. Yet why, I wondered, did nobody seem to consider it important to warm up and prepare properly for eight hours of daily work? Surely, the time my patients spent at work everyday was a more significant physical and mental exercise than the one, short hour a week that they were spending playing '5-A-Side' or a game of netball?

I decided that, if I were to be the best physiotherapist that I could possible be, then I needed to understand the working environment of each of my clients better. I wanted to examine how they spent the bulk of their time – what kind of things they were demanding of themselves physically everyday at work and for hours at a time.

At that time, I was fortunate to land a job working with a large manufacturing plant in the North East of England, at which a previous mentor and colleague was Head of Physiotherapy for the team of workers. I had tremendous respect for him, both as a physiotherapist and personally, and so I threw myself into my work.

I absorbed my lessons there like a sponge, improving my skills and increasing my knowledge of the physio field daily. To maximise my time there and further my growing expertise, I took additional training in Ergonomics and Occupational Health, spending time studying around my working hours.

Before long, my employer asked me to take on another of the company's clients – this time, a team working in a small food manufacturing site. Again, I launched myself into the role with characteristic enthusiasm; I made good friends and solid relationships with both managers and employees alike.

They began to trust me, and several months into my contract there they opened up to me with a concern.

"Ross, to be honest, we're not very happy with the way your company has been dealing with us. You work wonders for the team, but your guys overall could really improve the way they deal with us."

I was taken aback. So far, I'd had no reason to believe that the company for whom I worked was anything less than a leader in its field. What had been going on behind the scenes that I didn't know about?

"I'm really sorry to hear that," I looked him straight in the eye. "What's been happening? Can I fix it?"

He leaned forward in his chair and spoke earnestly. "Frankly, it's more a case of what's not been happening. And I don't know if you can fix it, but you might be in a good position to help us move forwards with them."

He explained that, in his opinion, his team had not had the level of service from my employers that it had been promised for many months.

"We can't match the budget that your main client is likely paying for your services," he reasoned, "but we ought to at least have the service we were offered from the start and for which we're paying, after all."

Clearly, he was feeling undervalued and overshadowed by the bigger, more lucrative manufacturer client. I asked him if he'd raised it with the account manager who dealt with him.

"Oh, I've tried several times to arrange a meeting, but so far ..." he shrugged and spread his hands in a hopeless gesture.

I nodded. So, nobody had been to see him and what had started as a small problem had now grown into a full-scale issue. I promised I would pass the message along, prompt the account manager or someone else to call him and to set up a time to talk face to face.

Every week, after my time with him and his team, I would return to my main place of work and relay the message.

"Listen – they're not happy. You really should visit as soon as possible – make it a priority. I think they might start looking for another supplier if we don't get onto this right away."

Nobody listened to me, either.

The relationship between my employers and the client deteriorated as their repeated queries and invitations to meet were ignored and left unanswered.

I felt flat, demoralised. Knowing that the client I was trying so hard to help was unhappy took the joy out of my work. What was I achieving here? I was battling a company ethos that I couldn't change on my own. Instead of leaping out of bed in the morning energised by the thought of the day's work ahead, I noticed a knot of anxiety form in the pit of my stomach as I joined the drudge of commuting to work. For the first time, it really began to feel like work – the unfulfilling kind. I began to wonder what career prospects I had with the company after all.

It never rains but it pours, as they say.

At around the same time, my old friend and Head of Physiotherapy was demoted as a new Head of Service was appointed. Shortly afterwards, my full-time contract ended as I requested different holidays to those offered.

It was clear that my time there was running out. I took a part-time contract with them and decided to start my own practice – "Therapy Direct Healthcare" – with the aim of being the best physiotherapist I could be on my own terms.

I started to treat private patients in their own homes, placing the emphasis on what I had observed in my younger days and finding out all I could about the work environment of each of my patients. Gradually, business picked up and, before long, I was working with several SMEs in the North East with between twenty to fifty members of staff.

I was thoroughly enjoying using what I'd learned and following my instincts. My enthusiasm for Occupational Health, passion for effective communication and skills in physiotherapy were all coming into their own, charging my days with fresh energy and helping me to recover my joie de vivre. I managed to get through the part-time work with my old employer with no trouble at all.

One day, I heard from the food manufacturing client for whom everything had gone so wrong. Word of my little sideline practice had spread, and they wanted me to come in for a meeting to discuss my submitting a tender for their contract.

Wow. What now?

This was not what I had expected at all. After everything that had happened, why did they want to work with me?

"What happened was not about you, Ross – it was to do with your employer," I was told. "We haven't forgotten how well you treated us and we'd love to see you back here. How about it? Think about it. Put something in writing and let's see what happens."

I was in a very difficult position ... my employer would be far from happy about it. I couldn't possibly tell him about this. I couldn't possibly pitch for the work ...

Could I?

I went to the Source of All Knowledge for help.

'I think you should go for it," my wife said. "This is a great opportunity, Ross.

This made sense (she always does) and so I submitted the tender. Within a few weeks, I was working with my old client and Therapy Direct Healthcare's move into Occupational Health was complete.

Of course, as soon as the news was shared publicly, my employer was not pleased. In fact, I was quite literally frog-marched from the manufacturing plant. Not my proudest moment, perhaps, but it was certainly one of my most illuminating ones. As I was propelled across the floor by two large men hanging on to an arm each, I couldn't help but think that this had all come about because of my employer's poor decisions.

I had learned another important lesson in business:

RESPECT EVERYONE.

Had my employers actively listened to the food manufacturer in the first place, this situation could have been averted. Instead, they'd lost out on a good contract simply because he focused too much on their larger, more lucrative one.

10 TOP TIPS TO IMPROVE YOUR 'ACTIVE LISTENING' SKILLS

1. Make good eye contact, don't interrupt and be attentive.
2. Remain in the moment. Don't lose focus just because someone else approaches. A good listener does not look over the shoulder of the person that's speaking, waiting for someone more interesting to come along.
3. Steer clear of technology and don't start checking your phone whilst they are talking. This is just rude.
4. Don't focus on getting your point across. This can seem insensitive. Instead, focus on asking good questions about the conversation.
5. Adopt positive body language; leaning forward and showing an enthusiastic, relaxed nature. Don't fidget, cross arms, look elsewhere or express inappropriate shock or disbelief at what's shared.
6. Remain open-minded and do not approach a conversation with prejudice, expecting to know what the speaker is going to say. It's amazing how much time is wasted when you believe you know what someone means without taking the effort and time to listen to them.
7. Care! We are all busy but treating everyone with genuine empathy and taking an interest in their story will make a big difference.
8. Identify areas of agreement with the speaker whilst avoiding statements such as, "I know exactly how you feel." In truth, you don't. Nobody likes to be patronised.
9. Treat what is shared confidentially.
10. Remember. This is one of the most important ones for me, personally. Remembering previous conversations and treating everyone with respect will help to grow the relationship.

CHAPTER 2: RAPPORT BUILDING

"Rapport is the ability to enter someone else's world, to make him feel that you understand him, that you have a strong common bond." **- Tony Robbins**

Having good listening skills helps so much when it comes to building rapport. They are so important to people in every walk of life; they should be taught at University!

The rapport I have managed to create with my patients throughout my career is specifically down to my developing good listening skills.

Let me explain: I have known technically brilliant practitioners who are better read than I, but whose patients seldom seemed to get better. These technically brilliant physiotherapists had not developed their listening skills and so had no real rapport with their patients. You cannot hope to communicate effectively without rapport.

THE NATURE OF RAPPORT

What is it, and why is it so important? The term is used often in a rather vague way to explain something ethereal – a state of relationship that exists between two people that cannot be defined.

The Oxford English Dictionary has a good try. It defines 'rapport' as 'a close and harmonious relationship in which the people or groups concerned understand each other's feelings or ideas and communicate well'.

It's that real sense of connection you feel with somebody you like and trust – either as you get to know them over a period of time or from the outset when you meet them. It's what happens when we 'click' with someone – really 'hit it off'.

In healthcare, your being able to build rapport swiftly and authentically is a skill without which you cannot progress. It's imperative that you are able to help your patients to relax, to trust you so that they can open up to you – not just about the pain that's afflicting them but about their lives too. The pain point is a symptom of something else that has caused it. In some cases, this may be a past injury. In many cases, it's revealed to be a repetitive action that the patient is performing regularly.

In order for you to find out what it is that has happened or is happening regularly, you need your patient to talk to you – honestly and openly – about his or her habits, job and lifestyle choices. While it might seem obvious, not all patients trust health practitioners easily. You need to be sure that the answers they give to your questions are true and full, omitting no details that may be important in your diagnosis of their condition.

The role that trust plays doesn't end there though. When it comes to executing a successful treatment programme, you need to have the 'buy in' of your patient. How can you be sure that he or she will carry out the exercises you prescribe them? This part is not in your hands; whether they follow your advice or not comes down to the level of trust you build with your patient and the desire on his or her part to get better.

It helps to communicate the 'why' behind the exercise programme you design for treatment. Your patient will be far more motivated to do the exercises if you can focus together on how his or her life will improve as a whole once the pain is alleviated. To find out what those deep-rooted, strong motives are, you need to find out what your patient wants to be able to do better every day: perform better in a manual job, pick up a child, run a half marathon. It's never enough to simply focus on the pain itself and to imagine it gone. It's more important and far more powerful a tool to help your patient to understand the real value of living a pain free life. If your patient trusts you, you'll be able to find out what those motives are and then create the most effective recovery programme.

No matter who you are, where you live or what type of business you are in, if you are good at building rapport with others then you will be presented with a multitude of opportunities throughout your career. Your friends, acquaintances and colleagues will want to help you to succeed; it's the natural reaction to rapport.

Some people find that rapport happens naturally with someone – you either have it or you don't. It's true that rapport can develop spontaneously in this way, but it can also be a learned skill. As it takes two people to create rapport – it is based on a mutual connection, after all, it is not something that you can create on your own, but you can certainly promote and stimulate it.

TEN STEPS YOU CAN TAKE TO STRENGTHEN RAPPORT

1. Carry on developing your Active Listening skills so that you don't run the risk of misinterpreting the other's point of view.

2. Spend time creating common ground in conversation together. Few people are entirely comfortable with what we call 'small talk', but when you consider that it plays a very important role after all then it seems less disingenuous. Far from its being

a lot of waffle and silence filler, small talk in the early stages of any relationship works hard to find the common ground between two people. When you can establish how you both feel about the weather, the latest sports results, a certain country to visit then you have a far better idea of who you are speaking to.

3. Ask open-ended questions – ones that cannot be answered with a mere 'yes' or a 'no'. As the other person is giving their answer, nod your head, remain open-minded to receive their opinion and sound encouraging.

4. Take one of their ideas and expand it a little – build on it, remaining mindful of their opinion.

5. There's nothing wrong with having a different point of view to the other person's. Rapport doesn't mean that you always need to agree with each other. Rather, it means that you are not afraid to tell them if you disagree or don't understand. It promotes the freedom of an honest communication of ideas.

6. Everybody loves to smile and laugh. If it's appropriate, look for ways to relax and improve the conversation flow with a little humour.

7. Most health professionals empathise naturally with others because of our caring nature. However, in order to build rapport with someone it's as well to exercise empathy decisively. Let the other person feel at ease by putting yourself in their shoes, knowing what they feel and by projecting a genuine understanding of how they are.

8. Be polite, friendly and generous, offering compliments if they are true.

9. Don't outstay your welcome in the conversation – know when and where to leave it.

10. Be conscious of your body language and non-verbal communication. You are giving away far more of your feelings and intentions than you know. Be open in your posture – don't cross your arms or legs, keep good eye contact and relax. Smile and sit up straight.

In fact, this last point deserves an entire chapter of its own. Research has shown that the spoken word accounts for just 7% of our communication. 38% of meaning is carried in the tone of your voice and the remaining 55% is conveyed in your body language.

CHAPTER 3:
BODY LANGUAGE

"We communicate at all times, even when we do not realise it. Be aware of body language". **- Pat Summit**

Rapport has a lot to do with rhythm. When we are with another person, we are instinctively aware of the other's pacing of speech, gesture and facial expressions. Achieving as close a rhythm of our own to that of the other person is the key to building rapport through body language.

Happily, this is a skill that is innate in all of us, to some degree. You've been practicing it for far longer than you know! Research has shown that babies modify their 'rhythm' in the womb, matching their own heartbeat and sleeping patterns as closely as possible to those of their mother. When they're born, they quickly learn another aspect of rhythm in body language through 'your turn, my turn' games. When somebody smiles directly at them, they then smile directly back. One gesture follows another, mirroring each other and creating a 'sameness' in gesture, posture and mood.

This is the natural way that body language can establish rapport - that deep understanding and mutual acceptance between two people. Largely, it all happens on a subconscious level.

Once you know how to read the signals that somebody else gives you non-verbally, you can exercise them consciously through 'mirroring' to strengthen the rapport between you.

How do you exercise your innate ability to build rapport non-verbally?

MIRRORING

It is no real wonder that we prefer people who remind us of ourselves. Every day, we 'mirror' the actions and body language of our friends, family and close connections at work. We adopt similar hand gestures, voice inflexions, ways of standing, sitting and so on.

It is not a conscious thing, though. It happens on a subconscious level and has been a part of our evolution over hundreds of thousands of years. Without it, we could not actively belong to our group, clan or family on whom we depended for food and warmth.

The tricky part is learning how to do it with subtlety: if your movements appear 'staged', forced or unnatural to your observer, you'll be found out and will probably lose their trust completely. Next time you sit with someone, watch their body language and start to mirror it. You'll have to do this as a very clandestine exercise, mind you; if they catch you awkwardly mimicking their every move then your conversation will be short. Do they gesticulate with their hands a lot? If so, use yours a little more animatedly too.

How do they speak? Slowly, with a low, sonorous tone, or quickly and excitedly? Try to meet them at the same pitch and speed of speech – again, making sure that you don't make it obvious. You don't want them to think that you're poking fun at them. Keep your mirroring gestures and facial expressions slight, concentrating on the conversation at the same time. It's not easy at first and may feel awkward in the first few minutes, but as you pick up the other person's 'rhythm' it will begin to feel natural and easy.

WHAT'S IMPORTANT TO YOUR PATIENT?

Of course, what you ask them is key. Sometimes, to truly motivate a patient to help him or herself to get better, you need to ask a specific, trigger question that elicits an emotional response. It goes further than "Where are you in pain?". Rather, it has to do with focusing them on the real reason why they want to be pain free.

What is most important to the patient? How is the pain restricting their activities, and how is that directly impacting on their life?

For example, a young man in his twenties with knee pain is suffering far more than just that. He might be missing out on playing regularly on Saturdays with his friends because of his injury – which impacts directly on his social life and psychological wellbeing.

Suddenly, the pain in his knee has taken on a whole new significance. Of course, it's your priority as you want to see him pain-free, but for the patient the pain of missing out on fun and feeling lonely is far, far worse.

Now, you have an extra tool at your disposal to incentivise him to do his physical exercises. Instead of asking him "How is your knee feeling?", you can ask him trigger questions that totally engage him emotionally. "How many goals did you score at the weekend, then?" is bound to have an enthusiastic response and motivate him to help himself to heal.

That's why it's vital to learn how to read the signs and use Active Listening with not just your ears, but your eyes, too. What are their words, speech patterns and body movements really saying when you put them all together? When you focus on them completely in this way, they will feel appreciated and respected.

In return, they'll open up and communicate more, showing you what really makes them tick. When you know this, you are in a position to truly help them.

How do you become a mind reader, though? Can another person's body language really reveal what they're thinking?

THE EYES HAVE IT

In studies carried out by American psychologists John Grinder and Richard Bandler, our eye movements show whether we're imagining or remembering a real event through touch, taste, sight, hearing or smell. What's more, the sense that a person picks to imagine or recall the event can tell you something of their nature, how they relate to others.

Broadly speaking, if a person's eyes move to their right when they're giving or preparing a response, they're imagining an event. They're making it up – something that they say happened in the past but didn't, or something that is going to happen in the future. If the eyes move to their left, they are recalling an actual occurrence.

Importantly, a person's eye levels show which sense they are engaging as they recall or imagine events:

Left and down

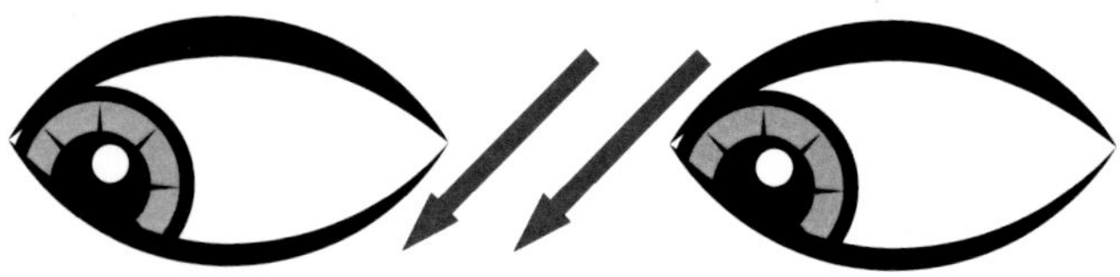

- Remembering an actual event and how they were feeling at the time.

Left and sideways

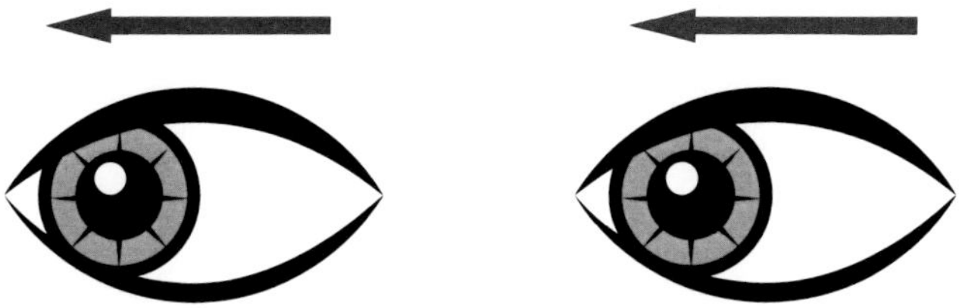

- Remembering an actual event and what they heard at the time. This is often accompanied by a slight tilt of the head, as though training the ear in the 'direction' of the sound.

Left and up

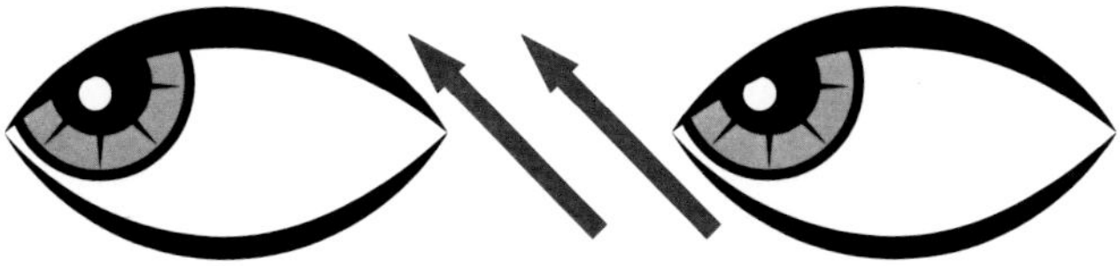

- Remembering an actual event and what they saw at the time.

Right and down

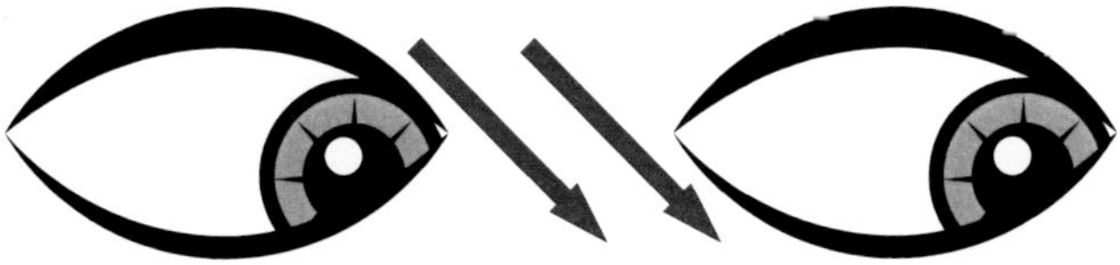

- Imagining an event and what they might feel at the time.

Right and sideways

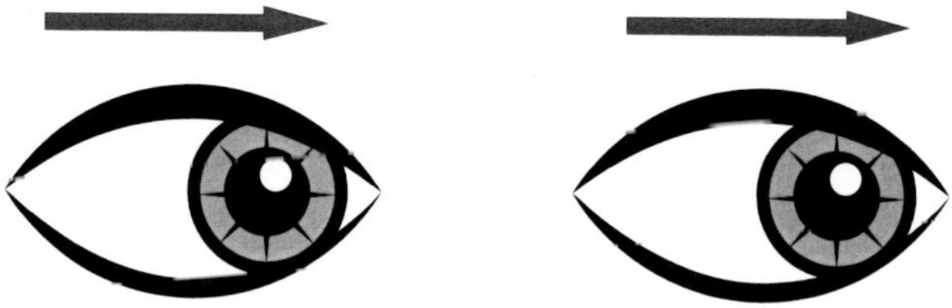

- Imagining an event and what they might hear at the time.

Right and up

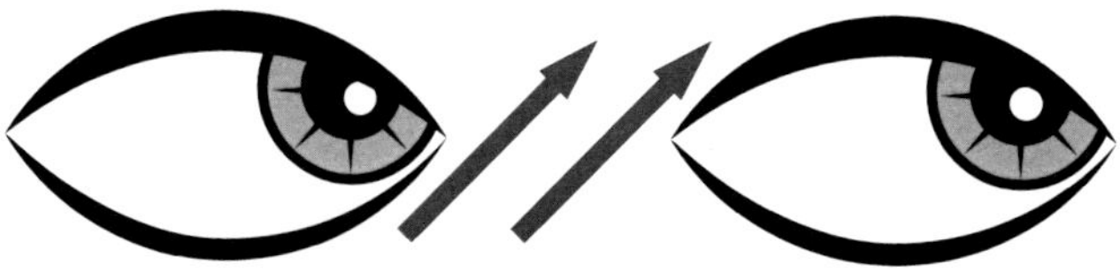

- Imagining an event and what they might see at the time.

An easy way to remember this is to think of the various areas of the body with which we traditionally associate our senses:
- We go with our 'gut feeling', hence we look down when we remember or imagine our feelings.
- Our ears are on each side of the head and on the same level as our eyes, so we look across and sideways when we remember or imagine sounds.
- Our 'third eye' is positioned above our eyes, and so we look up when we remember or imagine pictures.

Naturally, these eye movements happen very fast and there may be a sequence of several in a mere moment as a person's mind flits from one memory or make-believe scenario. You have to be observant to pick them all up, but just a couple should tell you how that person is processing his or her thoughts.

From it, too, you will be able to judge whether they are predominantly an auditory, visual or kinesthetic type of personality and so modify your communication with them. Phrases such as, "It sounds like you're improving …", "It looks like your social life is buzzing …" and "It feels like things are looking up …" can help to engage your patient swiftly when you know how they are likely to process their own thoughts.

WHEN MIRRORING SUDDENLY STOPS

After a spell of successfully matching your own body language rhythm to somebody else's, it is common for it to suddenly seem to stop. This does not mean, however, that you are no longer engaging on a non-verbal level; rather, it means that you've achieved your ultimate goal and have successfully achieved a natural rapport.

Old friends and close siblings can synchronise with each other without conscious or subconscious effort. They no longer need to mirror each other in order to achieve or sustain rapport and so their body language may not match. They relax and comfortably behave independently, showing a complete acceptance of the other person.

If this happens between you and a patient, you can celebrate: you have achieved that special rapport with this person through true Active Listening and are now in a position to help them on their journey, whether it's to pain relief or a balanced state of psychological wellbeing.

THE BODY LANGUAGE PHRASE BOOK

There are lots of clues a person can give you through body language that you can interpret if you know how to look for them. We've discussed a few; here are some others for you to add to your 'body language phrase book':

TENSE SHOULDERS raised, head lowering into the neck, showing fear of something as though they are trying to avoid a physical blow. Some people show that they are worriers by having consistently raised, tense shoulders.

BREATHING quick, shallow breaths in the top of the chest show excitement or anger. If the person is visualising something, they often breathe more quickly. Slower, deeper breathing that engages the diaphragm may signify that they are engaging their feelings. A deep sigh can denote a moment of realization or a sudden decision – quite literally an 'ahaa!' moment.

SLANTED BODY one shoulder up and the torso slightly twisted shows indecision, especially if they switch from one side to the other.

FIST even if it is held quietly in the lap, it denotes frustration and anger. A controlled person will be able to talk calmly and even laugh while the fist remains still – a tell-tale sign of repressed emotion.

FOLDED ARMS indignation or disagreement, although sometimes this can be a defensive gesture. In the latter case, folded arms could be protecting the vital organs from a perceived external threat or preserving their heat if the temperature is low.

TILTED HEAD a listening gesture – but not always angled to the other person's voice. It could be that they are listening to their 'inner voice' as the conversation continues in order to form their own opinion quickly and decisively, readying themselves to respond.

HAND TO MOUTH a spontaneous movement, usually showing that a person is hiding something, or regrets having said something.

WIDENED NOSTRILS an early signal of 'fight or flight'. The nostrils flare when we need more oxygen to prepare for sudden action. Apes use the nostril flare to warn others that they are preparing to attack; with humans, it can be either a signal of threat or fear.

LIPS a curled lip or a sneer however slight indicates the baring of teeth – a universally understood gesture of threat or disdain. Pursed lips show that words are being held back until an opinion or response is ready to be shared. A smile needs to be accompanied by subtle other facial muscle clues in order for it be genuine. If the eyes don't wrinkle up a little or the nostrils flare, this is more an attempt to meet social convention and acceptance rather than a reflection of true happiness.

FEET twitching or kicking show a desire to run away from a situation. Something that is happening in the environment is being perceived as a threat. If a person wraps their feet around each other or the legs of a chair, they are showing a need for comfort. Feet can sometimes 'point' to something – an object their owner is wishing to hide, or somebody attractive in the room.

CHAPTER 4: HOW TO TREAT PEOPLE

"I speak to everyone in the same way, whether he is the garbage man or the president of the university." **- Albert Einstein**

I have always had strong feelings about this.

I believe in making up my own mind about someone rather than listening to other people's opinions of them. When I was growing up, I believed that the best way to treat people was to treat them the way I myself would like to be treated. It's not a bad idea in itself; it's extremely useful and rarely has negative outcomes.

Now, though, I have a far better theory. I've realised that it's far more important to treat people the way that they want to be treated.

It all comes back to developing good Active Listening skills again.

YOU CAN'T PLEASE EVERYONE

Learning to accept that you can't please everyone is great advice – but it took me years to fully appreciate it.

So not everybody is going to like you. So what?

So life isn't always a bed of roses. So what?

So not everybody is going to agree with you all the time. So what? When you think about it, it's simply not possible for two human beings to agree with each other one hundred per cent of the time. If they seem to, it's probably because one of them isn't being very honest with themselves.

That's fine. It comes down to your respecting others – allowing them to have different thoughts and feelings to your own. How dull life would be if we all had the same views!

Don't dwell on problems or mishaps. If you cry over spilled milk you'll miss out on a gob-smacking observation: have you ever noticed that there always seems to be more milk spilled than there was in the jug in the first place? That's a far more creative response! Allow yourself some blunders and a little more childlike curiosity. Telling yourself off, or anyone else for that matter, isn't going to change anything. Lap it up (or get the cat to – she'll like that) and move on.

Taking everyday mishaps too much to heart can throw you off course. Don't let yourself be swayed by things you can't control. Accept the inevitable, brush yourself off and simply continue towards your goal.

Unless you decide from the beginning to respect yourself throughout your incredible journey, you'll find it very difficult to succeed. Self-doubt and procrastination creep in and the reasons for your not doing something gain traction.

"It's the wrong time to open a clinic ..."

"I'll start my business after I save a little more..."

"It's probably best to begin in the summer ..."

Even the best and most truthful excuse will never bring you success, so stop making excuses right now and decide whether you want to win or lose. I know this might sound harsh but there are no prizes for mediocrity. The media never raves about an 'average' new restaurant that's opened and the critics never herald the coming of an 'okay' movie.

If you wouldn't rush to either of these, don't expect people to flock to your clinic or business unless you are prepared to be the best version of you that you can be.

To do this, you must take responsibility for everything in your life. Stop making excuses, stop blaming other people, respect yourself and the decisions that you make. Commit to an action and follow it through until its completion. We deal with all of this in more detail in Section 3.

It all starts with self-awareness and self-respect.

RESPECT YOURSELF

Not everybody is blessed with enough self-confidence to feel that they can leap into a new venture such as starting a business and carry it off. Most of us battle a sense of inadequacy at some point in our lives and fear of the unknown is universal.

How do some people seem to breeze through it if insecurity is common to all?

In the same way you can. There are things that you can do, exercises you can practice to develop the skills you need to change your mental state from one of fear to one of calm courage. Exercise them daily, as you would your own body to bring it to a state of fitness, and your brain will develop new neurological connections – pathways of thinking that will help you to move forward.

The areas to focus on are:

- Visualisation
- Gratitude
- Goodwill
- Compassion

We'll look in more detail at the last three later. Right now, though, let's examine the one that successful business people and sports professionals swear by.

VISUALISATION

In his book "Your Brain at Work", David Rock outlines research that shows how repeated visualisation of a physical activity can literally alter the motor cortex of the brain. It is such a changeable, adaptable organ that it is constantly overwriting its 'files', reorganising and collating new material like a workaholic editor. It doesn't stop.

You can take advantage of this by using mental preparation techniques ahead of big moments at work. When you take the time to visualise not just with thoughts and ideas but with emotions and actions too, your subconscious mind will initiate a set of signals that can affect the way you feel and think. This in turn affects your behaviour, which of course affects other people's reactions to you.

If you could wave a magic wand and affect the outcome of every speech you gave, every meeting you conducted and every client conversation you had, wouldn't you do it?

Understanding the power of visualisation and the power it can have on your thinking and behaviour is akin to that. Learn to work your magic.

WORKING YOUR MAGIC: A VISUALISATION EXERCISE

This exercise is just one of many you could use to practice visualisation. There is no strict format, so research as many as you can online or in books. The main thing to remember, though, is that you need an uninterrupted space and to concentrate totally. The more senses and focus you can bring to the exercise, the better its effect will be.

- Firstly, close your eyes and relax. Breathe in for eight seconds, hold it for four and then release it for twelve. Repeat this a few times as you feel your muscles release tension.
- Think back to a time when you felt like a real winner; perhaps you won sporting an event, landed your first job or received a standing ovation.
- Listen to the sounds that surrounded you at that time – were people applauding? Was there music playing?
- See everyone's warm smiles, the blue sky, the coloured lighting … what did that occasion look like?
- Feel the temperature around you – perhaps the sun was on your back … What does the ground feel like under your feet? Is there grass or sand between your toes?
- How do you feel? Is adrenaline racing around your body? Are you laughing, do you feel the urge to leap around like a kid on a sugar rush?
- While you are seeing, hearing and feeling all of these things, immediately picture the scene that you want to affect. If you're going on stage to present a speech, imagine yourself there before that happy, cheering audience. If you're going into a boardroom, imagine yourself walking in and meeting everyone while you are feeling that glow of pride, warmth and confidence.

Over time, this type of exercise will show great results. You have probably heard people talk about visualisation and recommend it but the truth is that very few really practice it regularly. Just as with physical training to attain fitness, you need to keep repeating the exercise to see the results. Face it: you have nothing to lose and everything to gain from trying!

In case you're saying, "But Ross, I don't have the time for it right now ... I'll start it next week. I'm not in the mood – there's just too much on my mind!" then let me tell you that you can change your mood, too, in just a few seconds flat. Give yourself as much of a chance as possible to gain the good stuff life has to offer you: if visualisation has been proven to work, then surely you should commit to giving it a try – right now!

HOW TO USE YOUR BODY TO CHANGE YOUR MOOD

Just as your mood can affect your body – slumping your shoulders, hanging your head, looking at the ground, barely breathing – so your body can change your mood.

You simply reverse the process.

- Stand up and strike a pose ... one of a really depressed person. Slump your shoulders, hang your head, slow your breathing to shallow gulps of air.

- As you're standing like that, try to feel really excited without changing your posture in any way. It's impossible, right?

- Now, change your posture completely. Suddenly snap your head up, leap around the room, make some whooping noises and slap the biggest smile on your face that you can muster. Do this irrespective of the energy that you feel.

For the first minute it's going to feel forced, a bit false. You'll soon notice a difference in your mood though. Just as it's impossible to feel excited or overflowing with joy when your body is as slumped as an empty sack, it's impossible to feel depressed and sorrowful while you're leaping about, stretching and grinning like a loon.

It's true: sometimes you have to fake it to make it!

PART 2:
BE MEMORABLE

"I've learned that people will forget what you said, people will forget what you did, but people will never forget how you made them feel."
- **Maya Angelou**

CHAPTER 5: HIRING FOR ATTITUDE

"People may hear your words, but they feel your attitude."
- John C. Maxwell

If you are at the point where you are ready to expand, it helps to have the right people around you. In the early days, I fell into the trap of thinking that if only I could clone myself everything would be fine. I would be able to do twice as much work ... but of course, that would not have worked. Firstly, because cloning technology hasn't advanced past sheep in the last fifteen years, and secondly because for every strength that is doubled, so is a weakness.

The key is to find the right attitude in the people who compensate for your weaknesses and complement your role. In other words, hire the best people you can find and make them even better. Don't fear their leaving; rather, reward and recognize their skills so they don't want to.

For me, this meant surrounding myself with logical, process driven individuals because while I have ideas coming out of everywhere and I naturally see opportunity at every turn, I'm not very good at dealing with the nitty gritty, the spreadsheets and the structure.

So why should you hire for attitude and not aptitude?

Well, in my opinion it's because skills can be taught but

personality is more difficult to change. We hire on this basis and as we only employ senior physiotherapists the clinical skills tend to be already present.

This wasn't always the case, though, and we did once make the mistake of hiring a less qualified therapist whose attitude didn't quite match our own. The relationship didn't last and after a final debacle we parted ways having learned our lesson.

It wasn't the only time we made a recruitment mistake. In 2014, we took on a new administrator – more accurately, we took on the first administrator that we met. Wow - did our attitudes differ! Her idea of a busy day was to make three cups of tea and file her nails twice. When we pointed this out, she was adamant that we would never find anyone who wanted to work all day and then continued to send nasty emails for many months. Of course, had she applied herself as hard to her actual job while she was with us, we may not have had to terminate her contract.

These mistakes were hard to take, but all turned out well in the end. After all was said and done, we had a clear picture of our ideal team member: someone who understands our vision for quality and someone who isn't scared of hard work.

It was an opportunity for us to examine our core values and to make sure that we spent time finding someone with the same.

CORE VALUES

We behave according to what we believe and what we consider to be important. Our values determine our personality and when you find that your own values are similar to somebody else's, it's natural to find that you get along easily.

The best scenario in a working environment is to have a team of staff that shares common core values. It's one thing to decide what they should be – even to write them down, make a large banner and put it on the wall in the office – but if the core values are not demonstrated by your staff's behaviour, then it's unlikely that they will last long or have impact on the ethos of your practice. It's far better to employ people who naturally share common values in the first place than to expect staff to accept a list of made up values that do not truly affect them on a subconscious level.

When you apply this laser focus, you will attract the right clients and best staff as your ethos and vision is clearly communicated. Our vision has allowed us to attract team members from some of the largest healthcare companies in the UK along with a few from our competitors.

A team that naturally shares the same values behaves as one without having to plan or decide how to act. When somebody who has a different set of core values is brought into the team, that person's behaviour will swiftly disrupt the energy and cohesion of the entire team. Even if that person is highly qualified, has a list of credentials as long as his arm or has been the prized worker in your competitor's practice, if he doesn't share your team's core values on a subconscious level then you have trouble on your hands.

Core values in a practice or any business should be allowed to evolve as the business grows; it's crucial, though, to make sure that they don't change so much that your vision is altered. They are there to help keep you on track when your business plan isn't quite on track. Sometimes, what looks great on paper turns out poorly in practice. Make sure you hire for attitude first, aptitude second. After all, skills can be taught: personality cannot.

THE RIGHT PERSON FOR THE JOB

The best way to know if you have the right people around you is to keep up to date with your staff appraisals. How are they doing in their everyday work? How do they 'fit' with the rest of the team – or in other words, how do they show that they have the practice's core values at heart?

Measuring a member of staff's performance is a clearer, step by step process than assessing somebody's core values. You will probably have Key Performance Indicators of your own that you can use to evaluate your staff's performance. They should be clearly set out from the start in each individual's job description and raised as a matter of course in each appraisal.

How do you assess what a person's 'core values' are though? That's a little more esoteric; some staff members say one thing and do another, demonstrating their lack of integrity over a period of time. Sometimes, they might not even be aware that they lack integrity themselves; they might want to share the practice's core values as that is the image that they would like to have of themselves, but not realise that their behaviour doesn't reflect that value system at all.

The only way to find out if a member of staff truly 'gets' what the business is all about is to talk, talk and talk some more. With the team, have frequent discussions about the kind of behaviour that is good for the practice versus the kind of behaviour that is not. The clearer you can be about 'approved' behaviour the better, whether it's on the part of just one person or your whole team.

Of course, what you're aiming for is a team full of people who hit all of their KPIs and demonstrate your core values by their behaviour every day ... but as you can guess, that's not very realistic! People are people; we all have off-days and nobody's brilliant performance can be sustained without a blip here or there. If a person tends to perform well, though, and usually behaves in a way that's naturally consistent with your practice's core values, then he or she is going to go far. This is the kind of employee of your dreams!

If somebody neither measures up performance-wise nor demonstrates the core values through their behaviour over a period of time, then you know what you have to do. A misfit like this is easy to spot. Your practice must not be jeopardised by such a person; you need to work out an exit strategy with them. Think of it this way: they would be happier in a place that's better suited to them. You're not letting this person go because he or she is a nasty person; you're doing it as the job is not right for them.

It's the people in between these two extremes that are more difficult to assess. Somebody may share the right core values and yet not perform well. These are the staff members with whom you need to spend more time: perhaps they need a specific training program, a change of venue or a different job role. With a different set of KPIs, it's possible that an under-performing member of staff who has the right core values will grow and become one of those dream staff members.

If, however, you have somebody on your team who performs excellently but yet whose behaviour demonstrates a blatant disregard for your core values, you need to brace yourself and exit them from your practice. These people are the ones that can disrupt a happy practice; if a patient complains about service, it will more than likely be as a result of this person's behaviour. Remember – you cannot change personality; regardless of how wonderful this staff member's performance, the difference in core values will harm your practice in the end. People cannot change who they are inherently. Hire for attitude first...

CHAPTER 6: LEADERSHIP QUALITIES

"Great leaders don't set out to be great leaders, they set out to make a difference. It's never about the role and always about the goal" **- Unknown**

Leadership qualities are important whether you are sole trader or have a staff complement of a hundred. Your ability to enthuse, motivate and educate patients as well as colleagues and all stakeholders within your care is crucial for your success as a healthcare professional and businessperson alike.

Depending on which course you attend or what you read, leadership qualities number in the hundreds. For us, though, our emphasis rests on Composure, Sincere Enthusiasm, Integrity, Decisiveness, Industry Competence and - probably most importantly - Communication.

COMMUNICATION

The ability to motivate and educate patients through communicating and listening is imperative to success in healthcare but it's equally important when working with colleagues. Poor communication can lead to poor outcomes. Seeing as our emphasis is on quality and being the best healthcare provider that we can be, we work hard to ensure that we communicate well in all circumstances. As with many things, effective communication skills can be taught, but our preference is always to hire individuals with an aptitude for effective communication already in place. It's easier to train up and improve a person's clinical skills than the softer, non-clinical ones.

SINCERE ENTHUSIASM

Enthusiasm is contagious. Martin Luther King's "Dream Speech" only happened when he put down his notes and improvised from the heart. Elon Musk's dream and space flight, Richard Branson's genuine enthusiastic smile are all memorable because they are sincere.

Sincere enthusiasm, by virtue of its meaning, is impossible to fake. You need to become enthusiastic – switched on and energetic – about what you are doing, as it's your key to success with patients and colleagues. They're unlikely to follow your advice if they believe it's contrived. Your enthusiasm for what you believe makes you a charismatic, likeable character, too. It's easier for someone to follow you and to adhere to your advice if you are likeable.

INTEGRITY

You hear stories of people that lack integrity all the time – incidents of seemingly intelligent people taking credit for work they haven't done or placing blame on others for their own mistakes.

I wonder why it ever happens. The outcome can only ever be bad.

In my opinion, this sort of behaviour enjoys only short term gains. Eventually, colleagues lose respect for a person who lacks integrity.

DECISIVENESS

This is often the most difficult quality to master and one I struggled with the most. Your ability to make calculated decisions even when they may not please everyone is critical for success in running your practice.

Poor or delayed decisions can often lead to missed opportunities or unhappiness.

Practice this by starting when your partner asks you where you would like to go for dinner. It's a pretty safe decision to use as practice: wherever you suggest, you'll still be rewarded with a good meal! Catch yourself before you dither and push yourself forwards with an assertive answer.

"I'd like to go to that new place that's just opened in the middle of town. Then we can go to a late movie afterwards."

Guaranteed, your partner will appreciate that more than a watery, "I don't know, really ... wherever you'd like to go, I guess."

The truth is that the latter response communicates a lack of interest rather than a desire to be compliant and generous. The former more decisive response shows vision, interest and a desire on your part to create a vivid, happy memory with your loved one.

Who wouldn't respond well to that?

MANAGERIAL AND INDUSTRY COMPETENCE

Very often, people are promoted for being good at their job. While this is crucial for a business's success, turning a good clinician into a manager doesn't automatically make for a good manager. I have met some great physiotherapists who lacked some of the above qualities needed for a managerial appointment.

HR training companies talk about this all the time: a poor manager gives rise to poor practices at work and lowered staff morale. It's not necessarily the manager's fault, however. If they haven't been taught how to be a manager and given the correct tools to manage a team effectively, how can you expect them to do as well in that role as they did in their previous one?

Fair's fair: skill up your people by making sure they have the right training. If you don't have your own HR team to handle that for you, hire an external HR company to find out exactly what your team needs and let them deliver the programme.

COMPOSURE

"Life is ten percent what happens to me and ninety percent how I react to it." - Charles Swindoll

As they say, you can't always control your environment but you can always control how you react to it.

Lack of composure cripples your ability to lead effectively. This will invariably result in your colleague's lack of respect, poor productivity, poor morale and damage to your practice's reputation.

When you focus on your future goals, you will find that you automatically reach for solutions rather than dwell on your current problems. Include your team's leadership growth in your mid to long term goal plan, as your management team's ability to make good decisions is fundamental to your success.

For example, if a member of staff calls in sick and their manager simply relays the message to head office and HR, that's as far as the message goes. It's the easy option for the manager but it creates a ripple effect of ensuing complications that affects several people. Who's organising cover? Who's checked on the sick staff member? What's their prognosis and how is it likely to affect the team in the short to midterm? Which patients is it likely to affect? How many appointments need to be rearranged?

The solution-focused manager asks these questions on the first call, organises cover with sick staff member's colleagues, resources cover and only then advises head office of what happened.

On a smaller scale, a client may call and cancel an appointment or meeting and the business owner or clinician doesn't ask for any more information. That's fine, but left like that there'll be no further business with the client. Somebody has to make at least one more phone call or email to reschedule. By that stage, the best times in the diary are taken, double-bookings can occur, the patient is left waiting for too long a period to sustain his or her ideal course of treatment. All of that could be avoided in the initial phone conversation. The simple question, "When can you come in instead?" there and then would save administrative time which could be spent on more productive tasks.

By 'productive', I would like to be clear that I mean 'income generating' or 'brand building', which ultimately creates income. That, after all, is one of the main reasons why you're in business, right?

How can you find the most expedient ways to generate revenue with all of this decision making, management leading and patient care going on?

Read on ... you're about to get to grips with LEVERAGING.

CHAPTER 7: LEVERAGING

"Leverage is the reason some people become rich and others do not." **- Robert Kiyosaki**

This is the one lesson I implemented late in my growth as a practice owner. I wish I had made use of it earlier as it's one of the most powerful aids you can teach yourself and, if implemented correctly, it can help to make you more memorable to everyone that meets you.

I was the typical busy business owner, working every hour I possibly could to provide the best service that I possibly could. This often stretched to sixty or seventy hours per week and the only reason this didn't cause a strain on my family life is because of the unwavering support of my wife.

Outsourcing in the early days seemed preposterous. Why would I pay someone else to do what I was capable of? Surely that would be a waste of my hard-earned money?

I couldn't have been more deluded.

It took me a while to get around to making the calculation, but when I did I was shocked. I had been inadvertently losing potential earnings every week due to my stubbornness to keep all of the mundane, day to day activities to myself. If you are hogging the entire workload to yourself, you need to do the maths for yourself.

For example, if you charge £40 per client and see two clients an hour, your hourly rate is £80. If you are carrying out ten hours of admin per week, you would be losing £800 per week in lost revenue. If an administrator charges £20 per hour to carry out these tasks you would be £600 better off each week or just over £28 000 if you worked for forty-seven weeks a year.

Leverage your time, work out what your hourly rate is worth and outsource everything that amounts to less.

There are many tasks that fall into this category including marketing, credit control, purchasing etc. Look to outsource this to maximize your time and profits. The time can be used to see family and friends, keep fit, enjoy hobbies. Before we look at examples of this let's look at 'leveraging' in more detail.

There are various dictionary definitions of leverage but the one that's important in business is nothing to do with pivot points and levers. It is "the action in which you can get more done with less". For me, it's not all about earning more money but creating more time to use as you see fit. You could spend more time with loved ones, play more golf or even conduct more business, the list is almost endless.

Let's briefly look at the four most recognised forms of leveraging:

OTHER PEOPLE'S TIME (O.P.T.)

The classic example of O.P.T. is the leverage that exists in a typical job in which the employer pays someone to leverage their time (Other People's Time). They can get more done whilst using less of their own time. This is simply how the world works in the main; this example shows that leveraging is normal and happens every day all around you. For many years, I remained unaware that this was a viable avenue for me to explore.

TIME is the most valuable resource in the entire universe. If you lose your MONEY, you can always make more; if you lose your TIME, though, it's gone forever.

Some examples of O.P.T. that you might use include:

- Hiring staff and leveraging their time.
- Hiring a gardener or cleaner so you can spend more quality time doing the things you love.
- Hiring a virtual assistant in another country so that they can work whilst you are asleep as well as for less than a local personal assistant.
- Starting a multi-level marketing network or a network marketing business to gain a percentage of what your team produce. Indeed, it is no wonder John D. Rockefeller, a great American businessman and philanthropist said, "I would rather earn 1% off one hundred people's efforts than 100% off my own efforts."

A perfect example of leveraging other people's time is when you enter into strategic partnerships and joint ventures - but we'll talk more about these in Chapter 20.

Hopefully at least one of these examples starts to give you your own ideas for leveraging other people's time.

OTHER PEOPLE'S MONEY (O.P.M.)

This one sounds like the most fun ... Leveraging on Other People's Money (O.P.M.). I mean, who wouldn't?

The classic examples of this include raising funds from investors to grow your business or simply getting a mortgage from a lender to buy a house. In both examples, you use someone else's money to gain an advantage in return for paying back interest or a percentage of the profits. It makes perfect sense to make money work for you in this way.

When you start out you may not be in the strongest position to borrow money. We all have to start somewhere, though, and as your practice matures and you gain in business experience, you will be able to allocate your own money and time more wisely.

The key is to remember that borrowing to buy an asset magnifies both the gains and the losses. Taking an obvious example from the property market, if you put down 10% on a property that's worth £400 000, then your original investment is £40 000. If the property then escalates in value by £60 000 and you sell, you make a £20,000 profit before interest, taxes and expenses. The property only increased in value by 15%, but the return on your investment was 50%. Not bad!

Conversely, though, if the property drops in value by £60 000 and you decide to sell it, you lose all of your original £40 000 deposit and you'll have to pay back the bank £20,000 to pay off the shortfall on the loan. The property decreased in value by only 15%, but you have lost £60 000. That's one and half times your initial investment. Ouch!

When you use O.P.M., you will see big results one way or the other. Be careful to research your investments fully.

OTHER PEOPLE'S KNOWLEDGE (O.P.K.)

Robert Kiyosaki famously said, "Business and investing are team sports". It is impossible to learn everything in the world, so it's important to leverage on the right individuals and build the right team around you. You've probably already started with an accountant, a web designer or someone else you needed to help you get started. Keep these people close and treat them well as they are integral to your success.

Another example of leveraging with other people's knowledge can be your investing in a business or life coach, or gaining a mentor.

Learning from somebody who has achieved what you want is a wonderful way to accelerate your success, as is simply reading more books and listening to more podcasts on the topics you want to understand. By leveraging on someone else's experience and knowledge in this way, you can dramatically cut down your learning time and achieve your dreams much sooner.

SYSTEMS (INCLUDING TECHNOLOGY)

It's important to acknowledge the power of the internet and its use in leveraging. From moving away from paper records to cloud-based electronic records (EHRs) to a whole host of apps that you can use on your phone, healthcare has been revolutionised over the last few years. Modern technology has transformed the patient's experience of visiting a surgery or clinic, undergoing treatment and receiving aftercare.

As far as the health of your practice is concerned, you should make it a regular exercise to keep yourself updated and on top of the latest ways that technology can speed up your systems and simplify working processes for your staff. Educate yourself and see to it that everyone else working around you has a similar open mindedness towards the freedom that technology can bring to the practice. Indeed, blogging, e-commerce and/or webinars may also figure in your business plan for growth.

You'll find more ideas on how to employ technology for leveraging in Section 4, or visit www.the-ahg.com.

CHAPTER 8: OUTWARD APPEARANCE

"Your appearance, attitude, and confidence define you as a person. A professional, well-dressed golfer, like a businessperson, gives the impression that he thinks that the golf course and/or workplace and the people there are important." **- Lorii Myers**

Like it or not First Impressions count. Dress appropriately but don't forget who you are.

Although we'd like to think it's what's inside that counts, unfortunately first impressions do matter and especially in health care. As a physiotherapist, I can always be found in cargo trousers and a Polo shirt, a uniform we encourage in all our therapists.

Why? Well, we think it makes for a blend of good presentation and a casual air. Patients are often nervous enough when they attend a clinic due to the pain they are experiencing; we don't want them to feel on edge because we're dressed too stiffly, appearing intimidating in any way. Our stance is to try and make them feel more relaxed rather than increasing their anxiety by sitting behind a long table in a shirt and tie.

I'm not saying that smart dressing isn't sometimes appropriate; for instance, if your clinic was in the centre of London and your clients were corporate financiers or lawyers, they may welcome the similar dress code, but for our clients – indeed, I would suggest for most clients - it just doesn't work. It creates a divide that makes building a relationship more difficult.

Of course, if you love wearing a suit and it makes you feel good, then go for it because I also think it's important to be yourself. For me this became evident as I started to grow my business and began networking, attending tender presentations and contract review meetings. Most of the people I met, including fellow physiotherapists, were wearing suits.

Now, anyone who knows me would agree that I'm not exactly a 'suit' kind of guy. If my wife would have let me, I would have worn jeans at my own wedding. Looking at my colleagues and new connections, I felt an uncomfortable pressure to conform. I duly began to dress like those around me - and guess what? I instantly encountered worse results, fewer leads and less interest from one-to-one conversations.

How on earth could what I chose to wear affect my business? Looking back, I think I subconsciously put people off who must have sensed my discomfort. Fortunately, I realised quickly and reverted to me just 'being me' again: smart jeans and shirt with boots or occasionally smart trainers. It's who I am. I'm more creative, more productive and more approachable probably because I'm more relaxed.

I don't know if there's any research that's been done to back up my theory, and it certainly sounds strange that my feeling more relaxed because of what I was wearing could make such a tangible difference. But even when I sit at a conference table with ten other people in suits, it's as true today as it was back then.

I think it boils down to being truthful with yourself. After all, how can you create new and strong relationships when you start by being disingenuous with yourself and everyone else in the room? When you add great communication with an honest, outward appearance, it results in you successfully creating a more lasting, positive impression. You're practicing Being Memorable.

FIRST IMPRESSIONS LAST

Earlier, we looked in depth at body language and the role it plays in establishing that all-important rapport with others. While it is certainly one of the most powerful ways in which we convey and pick up 'impressions' of other people, the very first impression that you make is with your outward appearance. What you wear gives another individual their first key insight into you as a person – possibly because clothing can be seen from further away than the more subtle nuances of body language.

As it's true that people tend to like people who are like them, it might make sense to dress similarly to the people that you would like to impress. However, if their dress code is so much more slick and powerful than your own, don't throw out your integrity with your Doc Martens. If you go too far, you'll be uncomfortable with yourself and struggle with just getting on with the job at hand as I did, all suited and booted.

You need to strike a happy medium here. It's been shown that people who dress similarly get along better and are more persuasive and acquiescent with one another. Back in the 1970s, students on American campuses were dressing either in a 'hippie' style with flowing hair and raised platform boots or the 'straight' style with tank tops, neat haircuts and more of a librarian kind of look. A team of researchers carried out a test to see if fashion choice could really influence how people perceived each other.

They walked up to students on campus, sometimes sporting the 'hippie' look and at other times the 'straight' look and asked them for change to make a phone call.

The results were interesting: when they were dressed similarly to the student, the student gave them change 65% of the time. When they were dressed differently to the student, they were denied the money more than 50% of the time.

The point is, you can use this type of 'Tribal Wear' to your advantage in your business. If you are about to approach a big investor for a cash injection, have a look online to see how he or she dresses and perhaps leave your favourite baseball cap at home that day. If you're about to do some training with a room full of healthcare entrepreneurs, present the you that you are most comfortable with – within reason! Flip flops and baggy shorts might be de rigeur on a beach in Fiji, but aim for the middle ground and go for a groomed casual look.

While you need to be yourself, there's something to be said for the power of blending in!

PART 3:
BE POSITIVE

"Do or do not. There is no 'try'."
- Yoda

CHAPTER 9: THE POWER OF POSITIVITY

"You are the sum total of everything you've ever seen, heard, eaten, smelled, been told, forgot--it's all there. Everything influences each of us, and because of that I try to make sure that my experiences are positive." **– Maya Angelou**

Who hasn't heard about the 'Power of Positive Thinking'? There are a multitude of books and films about it – and if you're reading this, my guess is that you've already tried out 'manifesting' as it's explained in Rhonda Byrne's "The Secret" with varying degrees of success.

Quite simply, Positive Thinking is a mental and emotional attitude that focuses on the good, optimistic parts of our lives, creating an expectancy of health, wealth, happiness and success. Some people seem to be born believing that they can overcome any obstacle they come across in life. For others, it's more complicated than that and some consider the Power of Positive Thinking to be a load of rubbish.

I suspect that you are naturally optimistic, as pessimists tend not to invest in their own development by reading self-help books. However, most of us struggle to some degree with training ourselves to be positive thinkers, so read on.

SOME POSITIVE NEWS

The good news is that Positive Thinking isn't something that you have to be born with. Rather, it's a lifestyle choice – one that you can make. You can decide whether you want to be positive or negative in your thinking. It's worth keeping in mind that someone who anticipates failure is very likely to meet it, while things change for people who anticipate success.

In my experience, positivity breeds success. That's why we chose it as one of our company's Core Values. It's contagious and can improve the lives of everyone around. It inspires patients, motivate colleagues and kickstart careers. We aim for positive, solution-focused ideas to keep our patients and clients happy.

Motivational speaker Jim Rohn said that "we are the average of the five people we spend the most time with." I agree. Spending time with others is the easiest way to influence your own thinking; when we socialise with others, our train of thought, body language, rhythms and beliefs alter to mirror those of our companions.

This happens without effort on a subconscious level. It makes sense then, to make sure that we spend time with positive, successful and happy people! One clever way to do this is to find yourself a mentor. Mentors and business coaches are more available these days, as more people are aware of the power of sharing their skills. Not all mentors charge for their input: you may be able to trade your own knowledge and skills with them for their guiding advice. Your skills are valuable, remember, and someone who is able to help you may be in need of them.

In 2006, I was fortunate to meet Carole Beverley who was one of my very first patients. She helped me to focus on and achieve my goal of making £6000 in my first year. As the former Commercial Director of Adidas and Newcastle United, she stood by me during my early years and was indispensable to me as a sounding board. She's still in my life today as one of the most beautiful, dynamic and humble human beings I have ever had the pleasure of knowing.

Since meeting Carole, I've spent time with numerous MDs, CEOs and multimillionaires who have had a positive impact on my approach to life and business, not the least of whom is the former Chief Executive of Newcastle United and partner at PWC, David Stonehouse. His knowledge and wisdom have been immeasurably helpful in shaping my outlook and attitude. I am lucky to be able to call him a friend and mentor.

Managers and leaders who practice positive thinking tend to build a positive self-image in those in their company. They realise that personal and business success is rooted in one's attitude and thought processes. Remember, as Henry Ford said:
"If you think you can do a thing or think you can't do a thing, you're right."

The repetition of thoughts tends to lead to their manifestation simply because we are taking action on them. That's why it's so important to for us to be careful about the thoughts we entertain and to remain positive so that we enable ourselves to take positive action and so to end up with desirable results.

It is your mind that creates the kind of life you live. If you think positively, you will transform your life accordingly. Give yourself the best chance of achieving that as possible and find a good mentor. Your self-confidence and motivation will grow naturally as your successes multiply – whether big or small.

PRACTICING POSITIVE THINKING IN THE WORKPLACE

Here's a sobering thought: on average, you spend about a third of your life at work. That's seven to eight hours a day focusing on putting food on the table and paying for your lifestyle.

You have to agree, that's a good reason why you should enjoy working! Positive Thinking at work is extremely important not just for you but for your colleagues, clients and partners too. When you have a positive attitude, you transfer a feeling of success and happiness to others. Your energy and enthusiasm affect the moods, thoughts and feelings of those around you; they, in turn, feel good towards you and are more willing to help you.

Successful leaders cultivate a positive and inspiring workplace culture. They know how to set the tone and bring an attitude that motivates their staff and colleagues to take action. As such, they are likeable, respected and strong-willed. They don't allow failures to disrupt momentum. A positive attitude in the workplace improves communication, morale and teamwork – all of which leads to increased productivity.

When you start your own practice, the excitement of working for yourself can become all-consuming; you feel driven, energised and happy. What really is happiness though? It's easy to allow yourself to fall into the trap of feeling that you have to work to be happy. Addiction to work is the same as an addiction to anything else: a sudden, uplifting surge of dopamine that depends on the presence of a stimulus of some kind.

Do you believe that you have to work to be happy? If so, this is not the kind of positive mindset you should be trying to establish. Your happiness should not have to depend on either circumstances or luck. If you believe that it does, you are preventing yourself from being able to actively take responsibility for your thoughts and feelings. Positivity is a decision, not a happenstance.

Read through the following statements and see how many of them ring true for you:

"I HAVE TO WORK TO BE HAPPY BECAUSE …":

- Happiness does not come naturally – it has to be earned
- Happiness comes at a cost
- I have a list of tasks as long as my arm (quickly followed by another one)
- Without feeling a sense of achievement I feel strangely empty
- Sitting down and putting my feet up for a minute makes me feel guilty
- I am a multi-tasker. People who are not are under-performers
- Taking my full quota of annual leave is optional
- I should be doing something all the time
- Time is constantly too short for me to finish everything that I need to do
- My friends start their phone calls with, "Hey! I know you're busy, but …"
- I can't remember the last time I had a long, lie-in
- Time off is reserved for sick leave (although I can still work from bed)
- My friends are my colleagues
- My spouse and children hope that they will spend time with me one day, sometime soon

If you recognise some of the above statements to be true to you, you need to take stock of where you are right now and where all this frantic activity and work addiction is going to take you within a few years.

The truth is that you are entitled to a positive, joyful frame of mind without having to do anything to earn it at all. It's what being alive is for. Happiness does not depend on good fortune or a desirable set of circumstances; it depends on how you interpret your moment right here, right now.

It comes down to Self-Acceptance: acceptance of who you are intrinsically, not what your circumstances say about you to others. Once you can accept this reality, you will be able to use Positive Thinking to your best advantage every day and help others to do the same.

CHAPTER 10: CHALLENGERS OF POSITIVE THINKING

"When I hear somebody sigh, 'Life is hard,' I am always tempted to ask, 'Compared to what?'" – **Sydney Harris**

While most people agree that 'Positive Thinking' can only improve their lives, anyone who has tried to practice it as a new life choice would have to admit that it's harder than they expected. Behavioural psychologist James Clear writes that it takes more than two months on average for an individual to form a new habit.

One of the biggest threats you'll face in your early days of Positive Thinking is lurking in your social life, in the staffroom and around the office water cooler ...

BEWARE THE 'MOOD HOOVERS'!

If surrounding yourself with positive people can improve your thought patterns and positive attitude towards life, then it stands to reason that negative people will have the opposite effect.

Pessimistic and negative people are not just draining: they're a direct threat for any fledgling Positive Thinker. My wife calls them 'Mood Hoovers' – people who consume your time with little productivity. These types will suck the very soul out of you, draining you of all positivity through their need to be negative and moody. If they aren't whining, they're not happy; if they are whining, they're still not happy. There's no pleasing them.

Your chances of escaping these people entirely are not very good as they're everywhere. You'll bump into them in all walks of life and in every culture. That said, there are some tactics you can use to defend yourself and those close to you at home and at work against their negative impact. Take heart! You do not have to succumb to their draining your very life force and dragging you down.

ELIMINATE OTHER PEOPLE'S TOXIC BEHAVIOUR FROM YOUR PRACTICE

It's as well to remember that it's other people's behaviour that is toxic – not other people themselves. It can be hard to differentiate the two, but try. Usually, a person behaves in a controlling or negative manner because of some past incident or trauma that has affected them. It's useful to bear that in mind but remember that it's not always up to you to try and 'help' them unless you're a psychologist who's been hired to do so.

For the most part, your duty is to recognise the toxicity of their behaviour and to move on.

When our company was a fifth of the size it is today we had only a couple of clients. We had plenty of time to super-service them both, making sure that their every need was taken care of and that they would come back to us with repeat business.

One of them, though, was so negative that we decided to drop them.

Yes, even though they were bringing in about half of our revenue.

They simply weren't worth the pain. We were being systematically 'mood-hoovered' on a daily basis. They spoke to us as though we were dirt and didn't value what we did for them. We were in a dilemma – a difficult choice had to be made between two available courses of action: continue with them and be miserable forever or drop them and move on.

Our decision was both difficult and easy to make. On the one hand, we were a small business and needed their money. On the other hand, we were a small business and didn't need the angst. Continuing with this toxic client was clearly the wrong path for us; we decided to act positively, to be memorable for the right reasons (more on that later).

LET'S JUST BE FRIENDS ...

In the early days of running your own practice, you will meet up with other people's toxic behaviour. This is a given and it happens to us all. One or two clients will make you wonder if you've made the right choice to start your own business. They'll sap all of the enjoyment and excitement out of your new venture in as little time as it takes them to rip up your first invoice.

What's happened? They hired you for your expertise and professional care, yet they don't value your time, your opinion or the extra mile you've gone for them.

Be brave, though. It's not you – it's them. Although you might feel that you need to endure the abuse to pay the rent or your team's payroll, the truth is that you will end up worse off if you continue to allow this dead weight to drag your practice down. Wasting time on somebody who is wasting yours is costing you more than the hours you spend with them: it's also costing you the opportunity to start working with better clients.

If you want your business to succeed, you need to eliminate the poison, heal quickly and be reminded of what you need to avoid every time you see the scar.

You need to be able to identify toxic clients in order to avoid them in future.

HOW TO IDENTIFY A TOXIC CLIENT

Before you read through this list and gaily place a hoity-toity tick next to each point, consider that it is not advisable to 'axe' a client if one or more of these issues has arisen only once. You are looking for a pattern of toxic behaviour here, not a recent, first-time crime.

- **'SCOPE CREEP'**

Very often, a client who continually asks you to do more than you agreed to do for the cost involved simply doesn't understand your processes. If this is the case, keep timesheets and a paper trail of correspondence from the start that you can use to justify your position. Don't set a precedent of doing too much for too little money just to keep them happy in the early days as they'll understandably expect you to do it again.

However, if a client consistently expects you to do more or give more time to a project than you agreed, this will cost you and your team the opportunity to add better paying clients to your portfolio. Acknowledge his or her need for more time than you can offer and ask for a retainer – rolling over the hours he pays for from month to month so that your time is properly paid. If that isn't feasible, break the project down into separate phases, making sure that the process involved is clearly outlined in each agreement.

If the client rejects both of these options, consider it time to end the relationship.

- **COST-ANCHORED CLIENTS**

So you agreed a price in your kindergarten-practice days with a client that was lower than low, and now he's insisting that you stick to it. Times have changed, your business has picked up – but it won't pick up anymore if you keep agreeing to his cheapo demands.

If you've pointed out that your rates have changed and your client is threatening to leave, don't be afraid to let him. Ask yourself, "What will it cost me to have this client leave?" If the answer is, "More time to spend on better-paying clients who want my services", then you know what to do. Make sure that you either have several good prospects lined up to absorb the loss or at least a decent marketing plan with a way to measure the results in place.

- **LATE PAYMENTS**

There's nothing more frustrating than this particular toxic behaviour. Unless you have a large debt-collector there's not much you can do about it save go to court, if it's worth it. It seldom is. The best way to prevent this happening is to state your terms firmly and clearly before you take on the work.

Does your website have a Terms & Conditions page? Do you refer to it in both your agreement and your invoice? Some practitioners include a small print section in their agreement which runs to thousands of words – a recognised legal document but one that will go unread in all likelihood.

Make sure that you verbalise your terms prior to agreeing to take work on and that you allude regularly to your current Ts & Cs. Service industries can be killed off by larger companies' 60 or 90-day terms commonly held with their suppliers. You are not a part of their supply chain: you are an independent service. If you have a client that operates with these rules there is no reason why you should have to conform to them too. State your own terms and if you doubt that they'll be met, insist on a deposit upfront.

- **"I KNOW BETTER THAN YOU"**

This is the kind of toxic behaviour that will leave you smarting. You have clients and patients who respect your years of expertise, and yet this one always 'knows better'.

You can only help one client at a time on any given day, and as you will never have the chance to live a day twice, better to spend your time helping someone who takes your advice.

Even though he might pay on time, appear on time and rebook your time well in advance, is he worth it? If he's not accepting your advice and expertise, he's not going to get better. He's wasting both your time and his, not to mention his money. If nothing you do will satisfy him then he'll never 'see' the results he wants. If you can carry on dealing with the person who knows better than you, fine; if you're feeling depleted and disrespected though, perhaps it's time to end the relationship.

FIGHTING NEGATIVITY WITH POSITIVITY

In the same way that you can observe people's truth by watching and understanding their body language, you can get to know yours by 'listening' more closely to the thoughts that you entertain.

Your inner dialogue can act as your best friend or your worst enemy. What you tell yourself repeatedly becomes your reality, with your subconscious mind programmed according to your beliefs. It's important to tell yourself the right things – positive things, through affirmation or 'reframing'.

Put simply, to 'reframe' you need to swap a negative thought for a positive one. For example, instead of telling yourself, "I'm too busy", tell yourself "I have a multitude of options". Similarly, when you find yourself apologising for no valid reason to someone, surprise them with a positive response, for example, "I'm sorry you were expecting me to call you on your birthday" changes neatly to "Thank you for thinking of me on your birthday!" Some may argue that this is passive aggression; I prefer to think of it as Positive Progression.

Don't put yourself down or let anyone else do so. Avoid negative talk as it's destructive and leads to negative outcomes. You and those close to you are too valuable for that.

CHAPTER 11: EMOTIONAL INTELLIGENCE

"Life is 10% what happens to us and 90% how we react to it."
– Dennis P. Kimbro

Emotional intelligence (EI) refers to someone's ability to perceive, understand, control and manage their own feelings and emotions. It is one of the most important skills that you can have in today's business world.

Individuals with high EI hold a practical understanding of their own self-worth, strengths and weaknesses. In workplaces, managers with high EI engage in constant communication with their employees and strive to build a strong relationship with them. Consequently, it results in high retention rates, greater productivity and employee satisfaction at the workplace.

Managers and their employees with a high EI quotient are better able to work in teams, adjust to change and to be flexible. With constant growth in the business world and the related growing technologies and innovations, EI has become an increasingly important skill to attain.

HOW THINGS HAVE CHANGED!

The old-fashioned, traditional style of barking orders and demanding compliance has slipped away. We are no longer in a post-Second World War mindset at work; the management teams we strive to employ are not the authoritarian, 'command and control' types that stepped out of the army just after a heavy stint in a warzone, disconnected from their own feelings and those of their subordinates.

Today, we recognise that people need to exercise a very human sense of fun, curiosity and inventiveness towards their day time jobs. Encouraging someone to think for themselves, problem solve and come up with creative processes is not just a wise choice; it's tantamount to allowing them their basic human right to psychological wellbeing.

Some business coaches espouse that there is no 'right or wrong' way to manage a team: the authoritarian style can achieve as many positive results as the motivational one. While that might be true in the short term, in the long term it costs an organisation a great deal in staff turnover. Who would want to stay in a slave-driving environment when the business's competitor is much more laid back in its management style? It simply doesn't fit with the way the Western world works today.

Encouraging a high EI at your practice does not mean that you're going 'soft' on your management team or employees mind you. The focus is just as much on gaining top results as the old authoritarian management style used to be. After all, if you don't have performance as well as a fun place to work, then all you really have is a party.

That's a nice idea, but your practice won't last long. As you work to validate your team, don't sacrifice their respect in order to give them a creative, supportive place to perform. Make sure that your team remains focused on the core values day in, day out, as you find a comfortable middle ground of motivational and authoritative leadership.

IMPORTANCE OF EMOTIONAL INTELLIGENCE IN MODERN BUSINESS

Everybody is different and having a mixture of personality types in an organisation is inevitable. It's also the starting point of the overall group dynamic, the 'character' of your practice that defines the subconscious experience of your patients and staff alike.

Not everyone is naturally patient, cool-headed and always calm. Into the mix will come one or two more impetuous personalities, wonderful characters who fire up the energy in your workplace and move the practice forward with seemingly no effort at all. However, sometimes these personalities need managing and perhaps extra training in learning how to hold back from making snap decisions, acting impulsively in an arena that requires careful, methodical practice.

If you have this personality type, take a management training course to learn the skills you need to 'look before you leap' and to recognise this tendency in your staff. In any form of customer-facing business, this is an imperative skill to learn. Just one careless comment or snippy word to a patient who hasn't followed their prescribed exercise programme one week can make him or her distrust you and set their recovery back, for example. One hasty, angry email in answer to a service provider who's let you down can destroy a key business-to-business link in your network in a flash. Learn to stop, think, breathe and WAIT before you respond to these triggers: you're in business, not in the playground.

It's clear that EI plays an important role in the following areas of modern business:

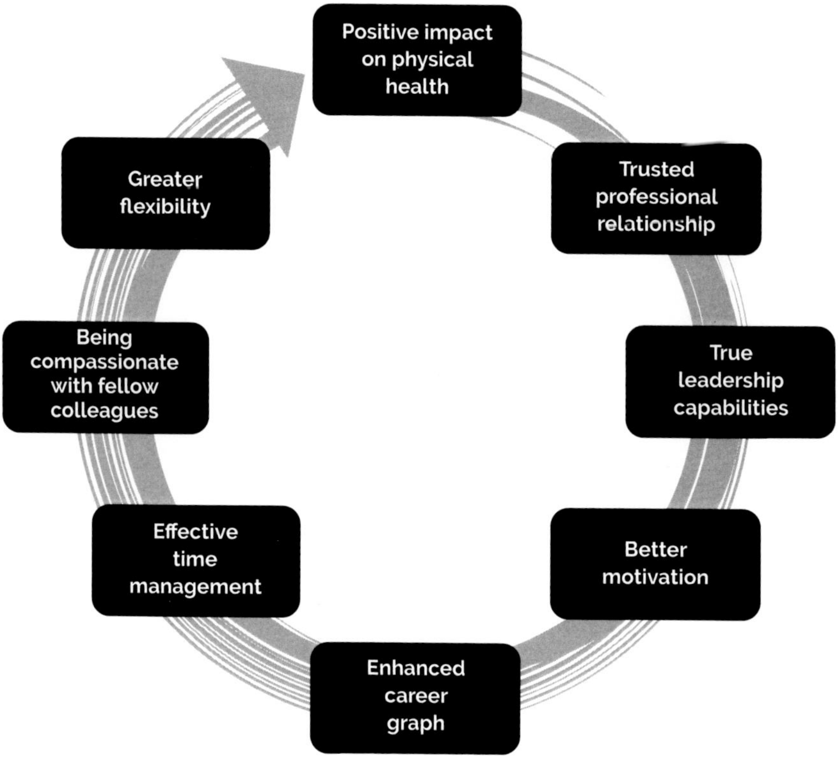

TRUSTED PROFESSIONAL RELATIONSHIPS

Maintaining good relationships within a business including colleagues and team members is extremely important. Various researchers have suggested that the value of such relationships determines the success of any business.

If a manager can manage his own emotions well, it is more likely that he or she will be able to understand and empathise with the emotions that impact the attitudes and behaviours of others. Hence, EI plays a huge role, from good leadership qualities to effective decision making.

TRUE LEADERSHIP CAPABILITIES

A manager with good leadership skills will see high levels of productivity and profitability. Someone like this has a solid understanding of human nature and exhibits a positive effect on their staff. Employees whose leader has a high EI quotient are motivated to perform at their best, not just for their boss but for the company as a whole. For obvious reasons, this has a significant impact on the culture of the organisation.

GREATER FLEXIBILITY

It is not sensible for any manager to assume to be right at all times and about everything. Flexibility with thoughts, discussing concepts and exchanging ideas enables employees to learn from each other.

You and your management team need to have an understanding that you cannot always be the most knowledgeable authority. If you deem yourself to be, then you're closing yourself off to change for the better. The less flexible the leadership, the more resistant the staff to new ideas from management.

BETTER MOTIVATION

Individuals with a higher EI in the workplace have higher levels of motivation and a greater ability to self-regulate. This can only lead to improved self-confidence and better focus on achieving long-term goals. Managers with a high level of motivation influence their teams to collaborate more effectively, to be able to adapt quickly to internal and external changes and to demonstrate fresh thinking and new ideas.

POSITIVE IMPACT ON PHYSICAL HEALTH

Studies have shown associations and links between a person's EI, mental resilience and wellbeing.

Someone with high EI understands how important it is to minimise and relieve stress in today's modern business environment. Health practitioners are perhaps even more keenly aware of the link between high stress levels and heart disease and elevated blood pressure. It can contribute to infertility, accelerate the ageing process and make employees vulnerable to depression and anxiety.

Having staff off work is every manager's nightmare. It makes sense to foster a greater EI among the management team as it creates a better quality of life for the staff. An improved social atmosphere at work makes employees healthier and happier.

ENHANCED CAREER GRAPH

When it comes to appraisal time, you need a strong EI to make important decisions. Who do you promote, hire and fire?
According to a survey carried out by Career Builder in 2011, approximately 71% of hiring managers said that they valued an employee's emotional quotient (EQ) over their intelligence quotient (IQ). In addition, 75% said that they would be more likely to promote an employee with high emotional intelligence. Around 59% of the managers said that they would not hire a person who had a high intelligence quotient but had a corresponding low emotional quotient.

EFFECTIVE TIME MANAGEMENT

A manager has the right to expect that his/her employees must meet deadlines. Employees with higher EI efficiently manage their time and complete their work successfully. With such emotionally intelligent employees in your workplace, you won't feel the need to 'micromanage' your employees. Emotionally intelligent workers know exactly how to prioritise their workload and to complete it in a timely and appropriate manner.

BEING COMPASSIONATE WITH COLLEAGUES

One of the prime benefits of EI at the workplace is the ability to maintain and display compassion for fellow colleagues. Compassion enables an individual to connect and interact with others on an emotional level, as well as provide great service and respond genuinely to patients' concerns. If your employees display compassion for each other, your practice will automatically become a better place to work.

Happily, it's not just the morale that improves; word has a habit of spreading and it won't be long before your reputation as a great place to work and attend as a patient will have travelled far and wide.

If you have a high EI as a business leader, you're in good company. Here are just a few astute business leaders who focused on developing their emotional intelligence in order to achieve a happy, harmonious place of work:

• Jeff Bezos from Amazon, whose self-deprecating sense of humour and conversational style encourages empathy, communication and self-confidence.

• Warren Buffet from Berkshire Hathaway, who once stated: "Success in investing doesn't correlate with IQ once you're above the level of 25. Once you have ordinary intelligence, what you need is the temperament to control the urges that get other people into trouble investing."

• Howard Schultz of Starbucks said that the main reason he came back to work was "love" for the company and its people. You can't ask for a higher emotional intelligence quotient than that!

• Indra Nooyi from PepsiCo once said, "Leadership is hard to define and good leadership even harder. But if you can get people to follow you to the ends of the earth, you are a great leader."

Summing it all up, in today's business environment, healthcare practices must develop their employees' EI skills in order to build up group cohesion. This would strongly influence both regional and global competition. Investing in EI development of employees will bring organisations in every sector more engaged, committed employees.

Reaching out for team goals is important; however, success at work, an ability to communicate clearly and solve problems swiftly requires the use of soft skills and EI. It's worth your working hard for the right level of EI in your practice: the related benefits are completely worth it for each employee as well as the practice as a whole.

CHAPTER 12: TAKE ACTION

"Imperfect action is better than perfect inaction." – **Harry Truman**

You've heard the old saying, "It takes a long time to become an overnight success." Unfortunately, it's true.

In the quest for 'mindfulness', counsellors encourage patients to 'live in the now'. Whether or not the idea of meditation or other exercises to control one's own thought patterns appeals to you, you'll have to admit: it really doesn't matter how long you analyse the past or hypothesise about the future as the only thing you can truly influence is the present. The here and now!

KNOWLEDGE IS NOTHING WITHOUT APPLICATION

Procrastination and over-thinking cause a lot more problems than taking action. Until someone invents a time machine, the past and future are just concepts that are completely beyond our control.

Worrying about a past event is a complete waste of energy; learn the lesson and move on. Similarly, worrying about something that hasn't even happened yet and may never happen is my definition of insanity.

The future gives us something to think about, something to inspire us and to plan for ... but it should give us nothing to worry about. How often do the terrible things we imagine about the future actually happen? In my experience, very rarely.

What's more, as you now know, I'm a firm believer that most negative events are drawn towards negative people and 'mood hoovers'.

If yesterday is gone and tomorrow never comes, we are left only with the present. When we truly believe and accept that, we're ready to take action. As Nike's strapline says, "Just DO it!"

Perhaps that's easier said than done. Most of us are prone to procrastination. Why do we put off taking action? How can it be that an entrepreneur with the courage to start a new business and dream such big dreams suddenly stops dead in his tracks, unable to move on?

IGNORANCE = FEARFULNESS

I mentioned 'mindfulness' earlier as it pertains to 'living in the present' – being perfectly aware of what is going on around you right here, right now. There is another meaning of 'mindfulness', though, which is equally as important to your approach to life and work: it alludes to your being conscious of yourself – your limitations, your reactions and tendencies of behaviour.

If you are conscious of these things, you are in a great position to improve your skills, learn from the experiences that life offers you on a daily basis. If you are not conscious of them, you will miss out on the most important lessons that you need to learn, not just in your everyday experiences but in your practice too.

Committing to learn as much as you can about running a business – with a particular focus on a healthcare business – is vital if you are to become conscious of what you don't already know. It is only by becoming educated that we can take on new ideas, think new thoughts and take action in new and exciting ways.

Learning from books, colleagues and mentors is the best way to empower yourself to come up with new plans to grow your practice. Without the input from an external source, you're merely waiting for divine intervention to show you the way forward. That may happen, of course, but it's a lot quicker to take control and invite new ideas into your consciousness yourself.

As soon as you become conscious of a new idea, you'll be able quite naturally to start moving in an inspired, new direction. Human beings are incredibly resourceful and inventive.

Any new "Eureka!" moment is worth celebrating, especially when it's backed up by an intuitive feeling that this is definitely the right way to go. It can change the way you think and behave forever in every area of your life, let alone the direction of your business. You are now able to actively decide which step you want to take next rather than just 'go with the flow'.

Being conscious of something new is the first step to growth; when you have learned something new and are excited by it - driven to try it out – you have taken your first step towards achieving real, measurable results.

The next step is a little harder to swallow.

ACCEPT THE BLAME

When things go wrong, it's easy to lay the blame elsewhere. If you're late to see a patient, you might blame your mobile phone for not reminding you of the appointment. If you lose business to a rival practice in the area, you blame the fickleness of your former patients for their wanting to try out a sparkly, brand new competitor.

Until you accept the responsibility for the adverse shifts in your life, you cannot learn from your mistakes and move forward. It wasn't the phone's fault; you should have checked your diary before the day started. People are not fickle enough to leave a practice with which they're happy; perhaps your losing business is due to your lack of preparation to offer them something new in time for your competitor's opening.

You don't have to beat yourself up about your behaviour when things go wrong. By simply acknowledging that things would have turned out differently had you acted differently, you are freeing your mind to make a plan next time. You won't be caught out again!

Just as there is freedom in your becoming conscious of new ideas and possibilities, there is freedom in your accepting the blame when things go wrong.

Choose whether you want to be a passive victim of things going wrong or if you want to affect better outcomes. By laying the blame at anyone else's feet other than your own, you are choosing to be ineffective, thrown about by changing circumstance. There's always something you can do, somebody you can approach for help, a new plan that you can make and then implement to affect change for the better.

TAKING ACTION

If you want to start a business, take the first step, whatever that may be. Draw up a business plan, approach a mentor, join a networking group. If you want more clients, don't just think about it, act on it now! Define your target market and get on with conceptualising a new marketing strategy.

Several well-known life coaches exhort us to never leave the scene of a decision without taking one action towards achieving its outcome.

Becoming conscious of a new idea is great; accepting responsibility for circumstances and realising that they are not beyond your control is laudable; if you don't take action on all of that laudable greatness, though, you're right back at Square One.

Nobody can make you take action, one way or another. It's entirely down to you. It's back to the 'accepting responsibility' issue again. Developing the habit of taking one step towards achieving your goal immediately after you've made a decision, though, is a brilliant way to fend off procrastination. Don't leave the site of a decision without taking a step towards achieving it!

If you're at your desk and decide that you need to put together a new marketing strategy to win back the business you've lost to that new practice down the road, haul out a notepad or switch on your laptop immediately and write the first draft of a letter to all of your existing patients asking them for their feedback on their experience with your practice.

Jot down a couple of offers that you could make that would gain their attention and attract new footfall. Each of these things need only take five minutes to brainstorm and scribble down – but when you've done it, you're a lot further down the path to success than you were five minutes earlier.

Taking action is powerful. Taking massive action will get you massive results, so make sure that's the kind of action you take.

I recently attended an event and listened to Grant Cardone as he extolled the virtues of "Ten Times-ing" your goals; I couldn't agree more.

If you want new clients and you decide to focus on local sports teams for partnerships, don't just send one email to the closest team to you. Send an email to every single sports team, hobby club and education establishment within a twenty-mile radius. If you don't get a reply after a day or two, send it again. If they still don't reply, give them a call or drop in. They may not be ignoring you; they may just be too busy and not good at time and energy management. If they say no, they already have a relationship in place, that's fine, wish them well and let them know where you are if they ever change their mind.

This can be summed up nicely with the 'Boomerang Principle': whatever you throw out there will come back at you at increased speed. If you throw positive massive action out into your local environment, positive things will happen to your business.

That boomerang's a bit useless stuck in your back pocket, though. If you don't throw it out there, nothing will happen.

Action. Without it, your wish for a successful practice will remain just that.

CHAPTER 13: TIME AND ENERGY MANAGEMENT

"Energy and persistence conquer all things."
– Benjamin Franklin

I personally find that routine helps me with my time management. Getting to understand my own personal rhythm in the early days of my entrepreneurship was hugely beneficial.

I'm an early bird and prefer to wake before 6am. I find the early morning peaceful and relaxing; it provides me with opportunities that are missing later in the day. Uninterrupted, I am free to exercise body and mind and find that my concentration is laser-focused. I'll often have completed most of the major tasks for the day before my family comes downstairs for breakfast.

It also provides time to exercise, whether in the gym or outside for a run in the fresh air. The rest of the day can then be spent with the daily workings of the business and reacting to the inevitable queries, safe in the knowledge that my key tasks are complete. I always experience a lull around lunch time and know that any work will take me twice as long to complete at this time.

To help with this, I stay away from our Head Office during the day although I'd prefer to be there for many reasons. I work in solitude for most of those hours as I find I am otherwise easily distracted. Later in the early evening, I get a surge of energy and often find myself reaching again for the laptop. The routine ends with my falling into bed by 10pm for a restful night's sleep.

When are you most productive? Are you an early bird or a night owl?

We all have our various rhythms but providing we understand our own bodies we can make the best use of our time. After all, time is the most valuable gift we have to give ourselves. Don't underestimate the value it holds and how much a short period of your time can positively influence someone else. We all get busy but we should never be too busy to help each other.

One way we can actively help each other at work is by honouring each other's time. If there's one thing that seems to universally get teams' backs up, it's wasting endless time in meetings.

SAVING TIME IN MEETINGS

Of course, we all need to have meetings during the course of a working week. How effective are yours? How long are they? Does every member of staff get there on time for them, geared up and ready to go?

If the meetings you're conducting are not efficient and effective, you need to cut down on them. Ask yourself these questions:

- Is the reason for having this meeting clear?
- Are the points we are going to cover set out ahead of time?
- Are all of the right people attending?
- Do we have a strict starting and finishing time?

If the answer to any of those questions is 'no', then postpone the meeting until every answer is a 'yes' instead.

Setting out the points clearly – creating the agenda, in other words – will inform people ahead of time about what they need to bring, what preparation they need to complete and how they are expected to contribute during the meeting. If they don't know these things, you'll simply end up having to call another meeting for when they've prepared properly. Don't let anyone off the hook: if they've all had the same correspondence regarding their share of contribution, not one of them should be a minute late (in fact, tell them to get there a few minutes early) and without focus on the day.

Coming with a plan for a regular agenda is a good idea for repeated meetings. When people know how a meeting flows and for how long, they are able to prepare better and bring their best ideas. They are in a more relaxed state although positively charged, as long as the meeting is well directed.

Every meeting should be aligned with the goals you have outlined ahead of time. It might help to have those goals at the top of the agenda, so that the attendees can see them and keep them in mind as the meeting progresses. It's easy to be led off course in a room full of people contributing to a conversation; use whatever means you can to focus your team.

An extra note on time in meetings: it may be obvious to everybody to set a start time, but it's amazing how seldom people remember to set a finish time for a meeting. The result is a long, waffly, drawn-out conversation that misses the main goals and takes over an entire morning or afternoon. Be strict about the start and finish time, and keep the meeting as short as possible by asking people to stick to the agenda and refrain from bringing separate issues to the table. If anything else needs to be addressed, it might be done via email or at the next meeting.

Learn how to control your practice's meetings as this is otherwise one area that drains the most time and energy from everyone involved.

SAVE YOUR ENERGY FOR YOUR BEST WORK

Time provides us with opportunities, but it's not the whole story. You need to manage your energy - not just your time - because managing your time in isolation does not guarantee your best performance; it simply guarantees you will be on time.

Time management takes you from absent to present but energy management takes you from ordinary to extraordinary in all facets of your life. If you want to be the best physio, parent, golfer or entrepreneur, you must invest the right amount of energy.

Most of us are short on time, especially when we're growing a business. Make the most of it by optimising your energy levels. If you're flagging and tired, don't try to power on; you're likely to make mistakes. Rather, change your state by getting up and moving, drinking some water or having a healthy snack.

Energy levels are not infinite. You cannot keep expending energy without the need to rest, recover and refuel. In sport, we call this 'over-training' or 'under recovery' syndrome, but it's just as relevant in everyday life. Try to prevent this from happening by taking on the appropriate levels of fluid and nutrition regularly during the day and getting a good night's sleep. High level athletes and sports people do this, so why shouldn't everyone?

Another way you can limit the loss of energy during your working day is by ensuring that you take regular gaps between meetings, staggering clients' appointments in a clinic to make sure that an entire morning isn't spent with the same kind of injury and technique. Variation and relative rest helps.

The likes of Jack Canfield and Richard Koch have written books and spoken memorably on the 80/20 Rule. If you haven't started to apply it to your business yet, then make it a priority to get cracking with it tomorrow, first thing!

The Pareto Principle, otherwise known as 'The 80/20 Rule' and named after Italian economist Vilfredo Pareto, says that 80% of sales traffic comes from 20% of your customers. 20% of your books are read regularly, whilst 80% sit gathering dust on your bookshelves. 80% of the world's assets are owned by 20% of the world's population – and so on.

For the average practice owner, 20% of your time might be spent as the leader of your business; however, the majority 80% of your time at work is spent running around doing tasks that you don't like, you're not good at and shouldn't be doing in the first place. Who said that because it's your practice you need to keep the books, organise the diary, come up with the whole marketing strategy, clean the bathroom and make the tea?

If that rings true for you, it's time for you to define your self-worth.

DON'T SWEAT THE SMALL STUFF

As we discuss in Chapter 19, you need to work on your business, not in your business. You started your practice, or are about to, because you love being a healthcare worker and you're good at what you do, right?

Without real insight regarding the daily leadership of your practice, though, it's very easy to overlook that fact that you're spending increasing amounts of time and energy on 'sweating the small stuff' at work.

As Red Adair says, "If you think it is expensive to hire a professional to do the job, wait until you hire an amateur."

What is an hour of your time worth to you? Later, we'll discuss how to calculate your self-worth and see, once and for all, how you're misspending your money by trying to do everything yourself. It's not just your time and energy that you're wasting by trying to be a 'Jack-of-all-trades and master-of-none'.

If you do your own accounts, write your own web content and never get on with what you're truly good at, you are costing yourself a lot more than you would spend on having a professional to do a better job.

Take a load off and hire professionals to take on that onorous 80%. That's what they're there for, and if you don't use their time you'll waste your own.

PART 4:
BE THE BEST

"Perfection is not attainable, but if we chase perfection we can catch excellence."
- Vince Lombardi

CHAPTER 14: CHOOSING YOUR PATH

"I can't change the direction of the wind, but I can adjust my sails to always reach my destination." **- Jimmy Dean**

Being the best you can be is easy once you've chosen to pursue something you love. When I was young, my stepfather would complain about his work, his boss and how hard done by he was. One day, I challenged him.

"If things are so bad, why don't you change jobs? Do something different or just get on with it and accept that it pays the bills and funds trips to Disney World."

He shrugged off my response. "You don't understand. You're just a kid."

Perhaps he was right: I couldn't understand his attitude at all. To my mind, you get one chance at this life and you're in complete control of your own destiny. If you don't like the direction your life's taking, change it. After all, nobody else will.

Years later, I heard the quote above which is now one of my favourites.

Remember, Your destination is easier to reach when we commit to our being the best we can be.

THE PATH OF ADDED VALUE

Do you want to be a 'Jack of all trades and master of none', or do you want to pursue excellence?

I chose to specialise in Occupational Health after having an epiphany during my fourth year of practicing. Why, I wondered, did all of my patients warm up before forty minutes of infrequent exercise but none of them warmed up for their daily eight hours of work? I realised that if I could understand more about work, the place in which most of us spend a third of our lives, I could give more value to my patients.

That added focus inspired me in my practice; it made me passionate about what I do and created a unique path for my career as a physiotherapist. It set me apart from my colleagues in the field and this feeling of being unique and needed in that area boosted my confidence and happiness.

Choose your specialism carefully. Think about it deeply in the early days of setting up your practice. Ask yourself the following questions:

- What do you love to do most?
- Who are the people you really want to help?
- How can you can you add the most value?

Once you've answered those questions honestly, you'll be able to make the correct decision. Work will no longer feel like work: you'll feel free to help your clients, safe in the knowledge that work is never a chore.

"Strive not to be a success, but rather to be of value." Albert Einstein

GOAL SETTING

Only when you have a clear idea of your chosen path should you set your goals. There is no point in setting goals and visualising their outcomes if they don't truly relate to what you do. You'll end up conflicted, confused and frustrated. When you're ready, set time aside to focus on writing down daily, monthly, annual and longer-term goals.

1. INTERPRET YOUR CONTEXT

Having a set of goals that you can believe in is crucial for many personal and professional reasons. It's important, though, to interpret your current context so that you can choose them accurately.

For example, a patient who attends your clinic with terrible back pain might not actually put her being 'pain free' first on his list of priorities. What she really wants to be able to do is to pick up her grandchild for a cuddle, or to put him in his car seat or pram without having to ask for assistance.

An inexperienced therapist might miss this. The most obvious 'goal' to set for his patient is to relieve pain. However, a therapist with the patient in mind will set a more personalised goal – that of the patient's being able to lift up her grandchild after treatment. This is the better goal to set as it incentivises the patient, increasing her chances of recovery as she works enthusiastically on her exercises.

Correct goal setting can measurably change someone's life and can be applied to business goals as well as personal ones.

2. WRITE YOUR GOALS DOWN

There's no scrimping on this. Write your personal, financial and business goals down, as committing them to the page helps you to commit to them personally. There's something about putting them in black and white that helps you really want to make them real.

Divide your blank page into five columns and head them "Health", "Relationships", "Career Development", "Personal Achievements" and "Wealth".

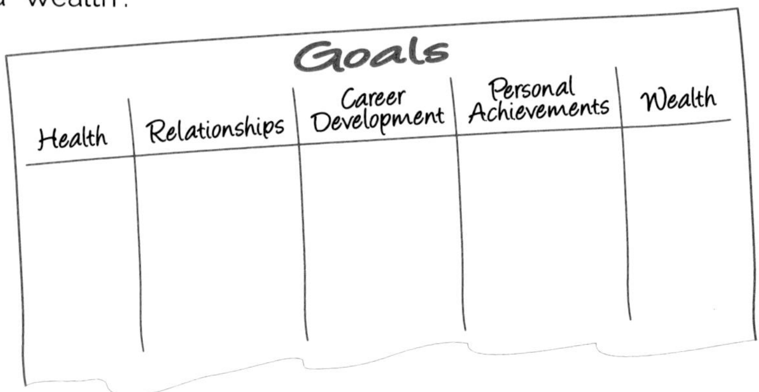

To give you an idea, my current goals include me being fitter next year than this year, being the best husband and dad that I can be, becoming a key person of influence within my field, climbing Mount Vinson in Antarctica and having a bank account with a private bank within the next three years.

My fitness is being measured by the time and distance I spend running plus weights and reps in the gym. I measure my 'husband and dad' goals by planning trips and counting the number of times I can drop my kids off at school and take them to their activities. The last three categories are easier to measure. When you stipulate your own goals, make sure you put in place some means by which you can measure your performance at the same time, or you'll never notice when you've achieved them.

It all seems so straightforward now that I've committed my goals to paper and can refer to them as often as I like. I'll admit, though, that this has been a relatively recent change as for many years I was too wrapped up in the running of the business rather than working on its growth strategy. These days, my vision is clearer, our growth has been accelerated.

WORKING IN YOUR BUSINESS VS. WORKING ON YOUR BUSINESS

For me, the ultimate purpose of a business is to free yourself from working in it day to day so that you can work on it. Of course, if you love working in your business day-to-day, do it! That's not at all the same thing as your having to do it through necessity.

If you're still unsure whether you are working on or in your business, ask yourself what would happen if you went on holiday for a month. If the answer is something negative, you are still in the business. I can tell you from long years of experience that working in a business means you cannot go on the same holidays your 'employed' friends go on and your paternity leave is measured in hours rather than weeks or months.

If this is you then I'd say that you are not a business owner but rather an employee. When you write down your business goals, bear the following in mind:

- Where is your business based?
- How many staff do you have?
- How big is it?
- What's your business model?
- What is your revenue?
- What is your profit?
- Who are your customers?
- How many products do you have, or will you have in the future?

Asking yourself these questions at the goal-setting stage will help you to measure your growth; it's the way you get to stay on your chosen Path of Added Value.

CHAPTER 15: WHAT YOU MEASURE IMPROVES

"If you can't measure it, you can't improve it."
- Peter Drucker

Once you have your goals in place, test and measure everything over time at regular intervals. Many practices fail within their first two years not because the health professionals involved are poor, but rather because cash flow is poor. You've heard it before: cash is king!

In the early day of planning to set up your practice, always overestimate your expenses and underestimate revenue.

Speaking to your clients and listening carefully to their responses is an excellent way of measuring progress. Take into account what they say on how you and your staff might behave differently, how you might embellish your services, what they appreciate about your practice and what they would like to see improved.

If it's appropriate, consider external accreditations such as ISO9001, ISO27001, SEQOHS which can add weight to tenders and set yourself apart from competitors as well as demonstrating your commitment to quality to your team.

All of this talk of change may seem daunting and perhaps premature if you're still in your early days of running your own practice, but take heart! You don't need to make massive changes to significantly improve your business results. Small, continuous improvements worked daily into everybody's routine can be just as helpful; small, positive changes made consistently can add up to massive changes over time.

THE KAIZEN PRINCIPLE

Kaizen is a Japanese philosophy whose literal meaning is 'change-good', in other words 'change for the better'.

It was famously implemented in Toyota after World War II by Dr Demming, an American who held that large, single step changes could be difficult to implement and disruptive to morale. He believed that small changes made daily to all processes carried out from the CEO to the lowest tier in a company were almost unnoticeable individually but accumulated to fantastic changes over a short space of time.

Kaizen states that perfection itself is not attainable or achievable but continuous improvements help us to develop and progress whether as a person or a business. In short, it is the process of asking questions, acting on the answers and then asking a new set of questions based on those answers.

This cycle of continuous improvement through evaluation repeats, motivated by the commitment and co-operation of everybody involved throughout the practice. Every member of your team is responsible for looking out for and noting areas of improvement – if it's just you to begin with, spend time focusing on every area you manage of your practice and jot down everything that comes to mind. You won't be able to make every change straight away, but by making just one change in each area to begin with you'll soon see fantastic results. They might even automatically improve some of the others you've noted.

Kaizen improves productivity, effectiveness, safety and waste production among other things. Naturally, it's easy to adopt a new philosophy such as this as an individual: you simply decide how you're going to start and continue, write down the small changes to the way you live or work over a given period of time and then get on with it.

It's more complicated getting the 'buy in' from a staff complement, mind you. As Kaizen relies on the co-operation and willingness of the entire team, you need to come up with a strategy to encourage everybody's engagement with it. Here are some ways you can encourage your team to take on the Kaizen philosophy at your practice:

- Learn about the process together, as a group. There is a lot of information available on the Internet and people outside of the organisation who can help to teach it. Invite them for a day's training, or treat your whole team to a webinar based on the philosophy, to help everyone embrace the new way of doing things and to work together as a cohesive team.

- Come up with a suggestion process. How will the ideas be gathered and shared? Do you have a weekly staff meeting that might be extended to allow for discussion? How will the notes be evaluated, and who will decide which points will receive immediate action and which might be shelved for a later time?

- Make sure that your system is clear. It's not enough to have everyone start off with an enthusiastic ethos only to have it dissipate within a month due its not being supported by a strong process.

- Reward everyone for their ideas. Without their ideas, you would remain blind to most of the small things that need improving within the practice. The more ideas you have to hand, the more you will see how the Kaizen philosophy works daily to alter and improve your staff's morale and working experience.

The Kaizen approach will help you to improve the way things work in your practice, but remember that without ongoing self-evaluation your practice cannot move forward in your chosen 'path of added value' as discussed in the previous chapter. Just as it is important that you focus on the changes happening at work, it is crucial that you spend time on improving other areas of your life on a consistent, regular basis.

SELF-EVALUATION: ASK THE RIGHT QUESTIONS

Renowned life coach, Anthony Robbins, speaks of self-evaluation, likening the human brain to the hard drive of a computer. He argues that whatever questions we ask ourselves, our brains will answer in the same way that commands we type onto the keyboard of a computer are 'answered' and delivered by its hard drive.

Because our brains store so much information gleaned from every experience we've had and resources we've stored, a request for a file is always met, even if we have to wait a little while for the file to be found. We have to ask exactly the right question, though, to get the results we want.

For example, if things aren't going well for you in your love life, you might ask yourself a question you'll regret. Imagine the dialogue:

YOU: "Why doesn't anybody find me attractive?"

YOUR BRAIN: "Well, you could lose about six kilograms, your hair's thinning a bit on top, you're getting bingo wings, you're driving a rubbish car, you're not using the right make-up, your clothes are so last millennium ..."

And so on. It's amazing how many answers to your direct question your brain will come up with. Ask a rotten question and you'll get some rotten answers.

It isn't being vindictive: it's simply doing what you asked it to do. It's given you a very real response to your exact question. Better come up with a better question - start hitting the right buttons!

Ask instead: "What can I do to make myself attractive to an ideal partner right now?"

Your brain will have something of more value in answer to that one.

"You could book a hair appointment today. You put the weights behind your bed a year ago – go grab them and do some lifts first thing every morning, starting right now. Nip into town later and ask the make-up expert to give you a free new look and come back with the right tips and eyeliner. Go online and see what car deals are available around the region – or find out about leasing a new model instead. Get onto Ebay and have a clothing clearout ..."

Just as many answers – but all of them so much more positive. Be very careful to ask the right questions! Negative self-evaluation is not only unhelpful, it's bad for your state of mind, too. Turn it around to a question that starts with "How can I ..." and see how many great ideas you come up with. Write them down, and take immediate action.

CHAPTER 16: HEALTHY BODY

"Take care of your body. It's the only place you have to live."
- Jim Rohn

One of the areas that will possibly need 'immediate action' is your own wellbeing: your physical and psychological health.

You cannot hope to achieve the goals you've set yourself if you don't enjoy good health. Unavoidable illnesses aside, we are all capable of improving our quality of life by making better, more responsible decisions regarding our health. One of the biggest, positive changes you can make is to cut out alcohol.

STOPPING DRINKING

In 2017, I stopped drinking alcohol for six months; my productivity went through the roof and my business doubled in size during that time. I resumed my usual, moderate drinking habits and, although I felt no different and saw no outward negative effects, the end of year review told a different story. I could see large differences in my decision-making – in particular, how open I was to my seeing and reacting to opportunities during my 'dry' period.

Opportunities are everywhere; as practice owners, they are our lifeblood. If we don't see them or choose not to pursue them, our businesses cannot grow. Personally, I think that most people either don't see them or choose not to pursue them. During the latter part of 2017, I fell into this; with hindsight, I attribute it to my drinking alcohol again. I performed for that period at a suboptimal level – I would guess at between 90% and 95%.

It might not sound like much, but that difference in my own performance had a direct and measurable result on the growth of my business over that time. I decided to stop drinking for a full year in 2018 – and it certainly started better. I have carried out several new projects and met my goals (including writing this book!).

I'd encourage you to take up the 'dry challenge'. You don't have to commit to a full year of sobriety to experience its benefits, though; start with one month and see if you feel the difference. I'm betting that you will!

For added motivation, look up Andy Ramage's books and website, www.oneyearnobeer.com. You might be surprised to find how many reasons you have to give up the booze, not the least of which concerns proper hydration. Such a simple concept, but one which many of us overlook. Alcohol dehydrates, and it's easy to confuse hunger with thirst. If you're tempted to nibble between meals, it may be dehydration rather than hunger that's driving you to it. It also makes you lethargic, which is not the same as true fatigue. If you feel yourself slowing down in the afternoon, drink water rather than coffee to rehydrate; it's a simpler, more effective way to beat the post-lunch lull.

EATING WELL

You've no doubt heard the analogy that likens the human body to a high-spec car, and how food is our equivalent of the fuel used to make the car perform at its best. While that analogy works on several levels, it's important to remember that your body is far more intricately tuned than any model of car you could dream of.

It seems to be a very popular analogy, but it does have its

problems. In a recent Facebook survey, 33% of those who filled in the missing word in the statement, "Food is ……" responded with the word "fuel". That's okay, but food is so much more than fuel, energy or calories.

When we focus on energy or calories, we're only viewing the subject of food from one angle. Of course, proteins, carbohydrates and fats contain calories that can be converted to energy, but food contains far more than those main components.

Mixed up with all of that are the micronutrients, phytochemicals, zoochemicals, water and so on. Perhaps it's more effective to use the analogy of a team of health professionals in a practice (with the practice representing the human body) to explain how food works, with each of the members of the team taking on a different role. They may not be the main players in the day-to-day running of the practice, but they all work together for the common goal.

Their interactions comprise the most important element of the wellbeing of the practice, or body. They're vital for the energy level, the performance, mood and long term health of the business.

Let's take a closer look at these crucial little cameo characters:

MICRONUTRIENTS: VITAMINS AND MINERALS

Without these, the body will break down.

None of these provides 'fuel' per se. The body can't get along without them, though. Perhaps the 'food is fuel' analogy is one of the reasons why so few people understand why they need a balanced diet, as it ignores the importance of the role that the 'non-fuel' cameo characters play in keeping us healthy.

We don't just eat for energy: there are a multitude of extra reasons why we need to know how to eat well. Your body is far more than a machine – Formula 1 or no. Every food decision you make sends an instruction to your body on how it should behave and perform. Make sure it stands more than a fighting chance to deliver top results – just as you'd expect from your practice!

A GOOD NIGHT'S SLEEP

Anybody who's started his or her own business or health practice will know the value of a good night's sleep … how much easier it is to get things done when you've had one! Again, I refer to the stopping drinking suggestion, as alcohol is one of the top reoffenders of disturbing a natural sleep pattern.

Did you know, though, that a decent sleep pattern can change your quality of life in many, tangible ways? Here are my top ten favourites:

1. Sleep helps to reduce stress
2. Sleep is a great antidote to memory loss
3. Sleep assists the immune system
4. Sleep helps to moderate blood pressure
5. Sleep is a painless way to help maintain your ideal weight
6. Sleep stabilises mood
7. Sleep reduces the risk of diabetes
8. Sleep helps to maintain a healthy heart
9. Sleep is a natural painkiller after an injury or surgery
10. Sleep promotes effective, quicker thinking

In the wake of all that (sorry!), why wouldn't you prioritise a great sleep pattern? The benefits are numerous and, best of all, completely free!

EXERCISE: USE IT OR LOSE IT

When you take control of your strength and wellbeing through exercise, you influence your health not only today but in future years too. This will help you to remain at the top of your game for longer, enjoying the fruits of your labour more fully – whether that means playing with your grandchildren, golfing or sailing in the Mediterranean.

The old adage "Use it or lose it" still applies today. Quite simply, if you don't use your body and keep it toned, it will stop functioning properly for you. It stands to reason that a healthy body is a basic requirement for you to blaze a trail in your industry and to enjoy your life to the full; however, our lifestyles are becoming increasingly sedentary and our future wellbeing therefore more threatened.

Technology is making jobs obsolete all over the world at a staggering rate, with some estimates claiming that up to eight hundred million jobs will be lost to automation by 2030. With an increasingly sedentary population, an obesity pandemic and the robots around the corner, it's never been more important for each of us to 'use it'.

Walking alone can help improve BP, circulation and help to strengthen muscles and bones. It aids memory, creativity and productivity by improving your clarity of thought. If just walking can do all those things, imagine what pushing your body could achieve!

I urge you to not make excuses and push your physical boundaries. I feel so passionately about this that I co-founded a company in 2017 designed to improve people's mental and physical health. Our medically led health retreats begin with a functional movement screen - or 'human MOT' - and progress to push delegates to try a variety of sports as well as participating in daily small group training sessions. The idea is that one of the activities resonates and they pursue this at home: the retreat changes from being a fun holiday to a life-changing transformation event.

So far, we've been snowboarding, paddle boarding, white-water rafting, canyoning, mountain biking and hiking. It's cool. Visit the website at www.the-ahg.com before you start the next chapter! Who knows – we might be adventuring together in the near future.

CHAPTER 17: HEALTHY MIND

"Everything is created twice, first in the mind and then in reality."
– Robin S. Sharma

Here's a question: when was the last time you spent a whole day on yourself, having fun, just relaxing or going on a new adventure? Can't remember? In that case, when was the last time you spent an hour purely on yourself, doing something just for the joy of it with no interruptions from anyone?

The vast majority of working adults in the Western world never bother spending time on their own 'joy level'. The most common reason is that 'there's just not enough time'.

The truth is that it takes just as much time to be miserable as it does to be happy. Happiness is not dependent on time at all. Happiness is a decision, not a quest in itself. You cannot 'find' it; you can only 'be' it. In the same way, you cannot 'find yourself'; you can only 'create yourself'.

This is really good news – if indeed it is news. It means that you can decide to experience happiness even when you're feeling frazzled with stress and lack of time. Hopefully, you've taken on board the previous chapter's advice and improved your diet, exercise and sleep pattern, which will go a long way to enabling you to feel less stressed and open you up to experiencing happiness. But why does it feel so difficult to be happy, if it's truly a state of mind that is based on decision?

SELF-ACCEPTANCE

It is easier to enjoy the rare, small moments of happiness than to feel happy all of the time. For most of us, a relatively constant state of happiness results in a gnawing suspicion that we're missing something, that things are about to go horribly wrong. Why is that? Who says that everything's doomed?

Robert Holden (founder of "The Happiness Project') has conducted many studies on people's attitude towards and aptitude for happiness. He writes that "You enjoy as much happiness as you believe you are worthy of, and you suffer as much pain as you believe you are worthy of." ("Happiness Now", Hodder & Stoughton).

In other words, it comes down to self-acceptance. How much happiness are you prepared to accept that you deserve right now? The lower your self-worth, the more difficult you will find it to be happy in this moment. Years of conditioning have programmed you to believe that pleasure is something to be enjoyed fleetingly, but if you enjoy it for too long you ought to feel downright guilty.

Happiness and pleasure feel great, but we have a deep-seated fear that to feel good is to be selfish. Speaking of something as natural and desirable as sex, Holden says:

"I eventually lost count of how many times I visited the chemist to buy condoms, only to leave with yet another tube of toothpaste." In our working lives, the underlying ethic of most of us seems to be about striving. We go about our days telling ourselves on an unconscious level that happiness must be earned, it must be deserved and paid for. Are you trying too hard to be happy?

The key to resolving this is being honest with yourself. If you are striving to find happiness rather than simply getting on with being happy in your current circumstances, you might be attributing more value to pain than pleasure. If you are, then spend that hour with yourself to do something you enjoy at least once a week, building it up to once a day. Start the reprogramming slowly, showing yourself that it's okay to feel happy – totally guilt-free – especially for an hour or two at a time.

You will start to see positive results soon after you've committed to the practice. If you're short of ideas on how to make yourself happy, you can always start with Self-Development!

LEARNING MORE = EARNING MORE

It can be said that your mind can be either your greatest asset or your worst enemy, depending on how you use it. Developing the skills to 'train' your thoughts and to keep your thinking positive is key to your psychological state and overall mental health. One of the ways you can improve your mind is to actively keep learning.

Accepting this is integral to the success of any practice, new or established. I would suggest that 90% of your focus should be 'industry' or 'job' specific for the pure therapist, 'management' and 'strategy' for managers and business owners with the remaining 10% kept free for focusing on anything else that comes up along the way. You never know where inspiration can come from.

There's a wealth of material from medical writers available to start with; you'll find a helpful list at www.the-ahg.com but it is by no means exhaustive.

SELF-DEVELOPMENT

Being the best goes beyond your being the best at your profession. Rather, aim to be the best version of you that you can be.

Read everything from books to autobiographies, listen to podcasts and audiobooks whenever you can.

I know what you're saying: who has the time?

Well, just as your patients must find time during the day to practice their exercises, so should you prioritise your own self-development. In truth, it's not more time that's needed in either case; rather, it's a subtle shift in thinking. You can find time in spare moments of your day without having to commit to a strict, hourly regimen.

For example, exercise doesn't have to be in a gym and doesn't need equipment. A patient may improve his spinal movement by side bending in the shower, leaning back whilst waiting for the kettle to boil or looking over each shoulder while he's sitting stationary at traffic lights.

This mental sidestep is equally important in your business and self-development. Time is everywhere; if learning is important enough to you, you'll find a way to do it. Get up an hour earlier, listen to a podcast in your car, read a book instead of watching television - the list goes on.

My personal favourite way to get more time is to avoid the news. I don't watch the news or ever buy a newspaper which caused an hilarious conversation when I was cold-called by a large newspaper recently.

"Sir," the eager voice at the other end of the line chattered, "I'm calling you as an avid reader of our paper to see if you'd be interested in our latest online offer."

He had just made what I hoped would be his biggest mistake of his morning. I cleared my throat and answered him evenly.

"I have no idea where you have found my information but you couldn't be further from the truth. I could not think of anything worse than wasting time reading about negative things that have already happened, that I can't control and which don't influence my goals."

Seconds ticked away. Eventually, a small voice responded, "I'll remove you from our list, sir."

I cut my ties with following the news in my early twenties but I've become increasingly glad that I did as the years have passed. I have found that, without giving my mind the unnecessary extra stress of carrying around toxic information, my business has developed as my focus shifted to a much bigger, healthier picture.

Remember: *"I am not a product of my circumstances. I am a product of my decisions."* **- Stephen Covey**

CHAPTER 18: MARKETING AND TECHNOLOGY

"Content is fire, social media is gasoline." - **Jay Baer**

The ways we buy and sell are constantly changing. When the internet ushered in online trading, the world saw a shift from traditional, personal transactions that relied on human relationships and accountability to price battles on a computer screen. Whichever website sold a product at the lowest rate won the business.

Ironically, the internet is now outphasing that method of commerce and is encouraging us to return to the old, traditional model once more. It's impossible to lie to customers online now as they can so easily research you, your business or product. The days of selling purely on price are gradually falling behind us and people are buying from others that they know, trust and like once more.

This recent shift towards conversational selling from conventional selling should act as your guide in deciding whether you want to compete on quality or price. It's one or the other: you cannot do both at the same time.

In the early days of setting up your practice or a business of any kind, it's tempting to start marketing your services aggressively – offering new customer deals and packages, presenting your 'elevator pitch' at the drop of a hat whenever you meet somebody new. Of course, you need to get the word out there that this is what you're doing now, but it's far better to leave a positive impression. Hard selling isn't for everyone and is possibly even less popular in the health business.

Concentrate instead on getting to know someone by using open ended questions, encouraging conversation and making it your job to get to know your customers rather than insisting that they get to know you. Avoid selling your product and services. Focus instead on giving a prospective customer what they need, rather than what you want them to have. This approach will create more opportunities for you in the long run. When you approach a company in the hope of establishing a new working relationship, ask what they need before you send over a long list of your services. That way, you can tailor your pitch to suit them better and stand a better chance of landing the contract.

ONE TO ONE VERSUS ONE TO MANY

Having said that, bear in mind that selling 'one to one' is fundamentally flawed: there's a very real limit on how many clients you can pitch to individually. Of course, building client relationships is key to maintaining working connections, but work on them after you've reached out to a wider market in the first instance.

Selling 'one to many' through networking, social media and collaboration is key to reaching more potential customers. In fact, the importance of social media was evidenced lately in a recent study. 41% of customers who responded said it's important that a business has a strong social media presence, 75% said they had acted after being inspired by a someone's social media post and 60% said they had discovered and purchased new products on social media.

To be clear, this kind of marketing is a far cry from the 'scattergun' form of mass marketing that businesses and practices regularly performed several years ago. It's not about putting your clinic on Yell anymore. Marketing through social media, networking and collaboration is about being creative and creating links. We'll look at the power of networking and collaboration in the next chapter.

CREATIVE THINKING IN MARKETING

Happily, the days of generic advertising and sticking to staid marketing rules of thumb are over. With the advent of social media, even small businesses and healthcare practices can afford to market themselves to a target audience and measure the results of each campaign.

You don't need thousands in the bank to fling at a television or radio campaign, hoping that your message reaches a few ears that happen to be tuned in at the time. With a little time spent on researching your market, coming up with a truly beneficial offer and asking for expert help in creating the message, you can niche target market yourself even on a tight budget.

Healthcare professionals need to be marketers too. Anybody in business has to be. While hiring a professional marketing team to take you from point A to point Z would be wonderful, there are some things that you can do yourself that will bring you positive results and help you to create a bigger marketing budget for a follow-up campaign.

You don't have to be a social media guru to set up a few key accounts to get started. Remember that just because you might not be interested in Twitter or Facebook doesn't mean that your target market isn't. You need to get in front of the people that you want to talk to: once you are on their media channels, you'll not only have the opportunity to talk to them, but crucially, you'll be able to find out what they need too.

What do they say about their healthcare experiences? What do they say that they want that they're not getting? What kind of misinformation are they reading or viewing on social media that you could correct or clarify with an ongoing blog or a series of articles? Become the go-to expert in this way and your brand will be established for good.

Once you have a functioning, informative website, it costs nothing to set yourself up with just a few important social media platforms. Facebook is the leading advertising platform currently, so make sure you have a group or page set up there. Twitter and Instagram can be linked to your Facebook platform so that all of your messages are uploaded automatically.

The most time-consuming part of the process is writing your updates. There's an art to getting your message angled correctly with SEO-rich phrasing, but there's a time-saving way to do that.

- Set aside a morning or afternoon once a month or once a week to write all of your updates in one sitting.

- Your updates should be less about what you're doing and more to do with what your clients want to know about – healthcare questions answered, comments on topical news items regarding healthcare and so on.

- In every case, make sure that your updates refer the reader back to your website. That's where your contact information is, along with your services and current offers.

- Invest in inexpensive automation software such as Hootsuite, which will allow you to upload all of your updates in one go and to schedule their 'publishing' dates. This frees you up completely from having to manually do it yourself. Your diary is yours to get on with business while your social media marketing ticks along in the background.

There's no reason why health practitioners cannot be marketing practitioners.

Take physiotherapists, for example. Physiotherapy is a crucial part of healthcare; physios often undervalue the skills they have, though, thus inadvertently pigeon-holing themselves. There are many areas in which physios can apply their skills, and it's up to each of us to look into the opportunities that are out there.

We're at a fascinating point in time where technology is moving so fast I can hardly keep up, healthy practices are changing with gyms opening on every corner and protein being put in everything. There is opportunity for you everywhere; as people invest in their health, they need good quality care. Talk to your local gyms, sports teams, running clubs – suggest to them that you can set up pop up clinics to help them. Ask to use their own social media platforms to advertise for you: it costs them nothing and will help them to increase footfall at the same time.

A classic 'win-win' marketing strategy!

In case you're saying, "Yes, but I'm no good at the whole selling and marketing game. I would feel totally out of my comfort zone approaching companies like that. They're probably sick and tired of being approached by my competition, in any case …" then remember: most of your competitors are held back by fear of rejection too, so the chances are that these companies haven't yet been approached by anybody! You'll be amazed at how many opportunities there are out there waiting for you.

TECHNOLOGY

Don't live in the past and never fear change, for this is where opportunity resides.

Technology is quite literally the future so regardless of your sector, learn, embrace and invest in it wherever feasible.

Just as with marketing, if you look around you and keep your eyes open for opportunities in technology that can help you in your new venture, you'll suddenly start seeing them everywhere. In healthcare, the future is wearables and remote care. If you're not especially technically minded, go online and start researching what others in the field are doing. Download a couple of podcasts a week that are dedicated to discussing the latest time-saving, problem-solving gadgets that are available. Get involved now or miss the curve.

Take watches, for example. Fashionable, stylish watches that do little other than tell the time are more frequently being replaced by wearable technology such as Apple watches, Fitbits and jawbones. Instead of just telling you the time and date, your wrist now tells you your blood pressure, how many calories you've had, how many steps you've taken and how many flights of steps you've encountered.

As technology evolves, I suspect the information will improve to provide even more specific health information, such as blood sugar levels or levels of hydration. The benefits are massive with 82% of wearable users in America already reporting that the new technology has enhanced their lives in one way or another.

A Fitbit device can improve a sense of belonging or community as friends and colleagues enter challenges to gain the most steps in their workweek hustle. I've found myself running up and down the stairs on a night time just to get to ten thousand steps or doing laps around the kitchen. It generates teasing conversations the next day with my family, and that's a good thing. It stimulates the feeling of togetherness. I'm all for technology that can do that!

Of course, you can extend these benefits to your patients and staff. Tracking data such as heart rate and calorific intake can be hugely powerful in someone's personal goal setting whether it be to lose weight or to improve cardiovascular fitness. It can also be a powerful tool when tracking sleep; as we discussed earlier, sleep is integral to health and energy management.

Devices that track personal health data can provide you with patient information which will enable you to outline and carry out a plan to assist in personalised care packages. You will be leaving little to chance; why wouldn't you want to invest in technology that could so easily pay for itself?

Invest in Intranet - communication methods to make conversation and collaboration easy for colleagues and patients. The easier it is to communicate between you, the easier it is to grow your practice and to help others. In time, as long as you make it your aim to be so, you will become a key person of influence within your sector and geographical area.

CHAPTER 19: NETWORKING AND PARTNERSHIPS

"Don't judge each day by the harvest you reap but by the seeds that you plant." **- Robert Louis Stevenson**

Business is all about relationship building. It's more to do with meeting people, venturing down new business growth paths with the right ones, being flexible and mobile in your day to day dealings and focusing on the future rather than on this week's paycheck, next week's or even next month's.

As I say, you need to work on your business, not in it. If your business is reliant on your working in it, you simply have a job. If you're serious about scaling up your business then you must engineer your exit from the day to day tasks. In my case, I needed to stop treating patients every day.

"Aren't you a physiotherapist though?" I hear you ask. Of course, but I'm a practice owner too. That fills up my diary just as easily as would my treating a list of patients. I made the decision to focus on growing my practice, hiring others to treat the patients while I took care of the business overall.

When you take that leap of faith and start to spend time on your business rather than in it, your network can expand exponentially. With your growing network comes all of the exciting opportunities!

Your NETWORK is your NET WORTH

It's astonishing how many practice owners overlook the power and pleasure of business networking. Since I started to network, my practice has grown in ways I could never have envisaged when I first set up on my own. Other people's ideas, support and guidance have helped me to find my path, let alone actually navigate it. It will do the same for you too, so adopt the mindset from the get go that 'no man is an island' and anticipate the joys of steering this ship with a full crew!

When I started my own practice, collaboration was a rare thing indeed. On the face of it, helping out your main competition seems counter-intuitive after all. Certainly everyone back in my early days fiercely protected their own little piece of the pie.

I remember approaching one physio practice and suggesting we could outperform a very large, well-known health insurance provider if we joined forces. Perhaps I was being overly ambitious – as that provider is still going strong - but we still work closely with that clinic and have helped them win their own contracts through referrals.

We've also been able to win larger and larger contracts as our practice and associated network has grown. Thanks to our collaboration with them, we are able to more easily demonstrate the pathways and clinical governance that surrounds our supply chain.

THAT 80/20 PRINCIPLE ...

Various books I have read over the years suggest you single out the largest and most lucrative contracts and clients. The much quoted '80/20 Principle' suggests that 80% of profit comes from less than 20% of our clients; likewise, 80% of the hassle comes from about 20% percentage of clients.

While I am a firm believer in ditching the toxic clients and negative people, I also believe that engaging with smaller collaborative businesses has immense value. When you find a likeminded individual and company to work alongside, your joint growth can be accelerated.

This has happened to me personally numerous times over the years with our largest current client starting out as one of our smallest and earliest many years ago. One of our latest ventures, "CF360", enables us to provide unique health and fitness retreats around the world. It only came about as the result of a conversation with a local personal trainer, Chris Morris from "Clear Fitness".

It was clear when we first talked that we had many similar traits, shared similar visions and had a similar ethos regarding helping people. In addition, Chris understands anatomy, biomechanics and nutrition. We are now friends and business partners looking to change people's lives positively worldwide. This only happened through our collaboration: two relatively small businesses partnering up and developing a relationship through mutual respect.

Who says you need to woo the biggest outfit there is? If you find a smaller complementary business partner, nurture the connection and move forwards together. You'll be delighted with the results!

DON'T BE A SPAMMER IN THE WORKS!

Networking is helping people rather than selling to people. Not everyone is ready to buy when you are ready to sell; if every communication you share is about your latest offer or package deal, you're going to create the impression that you're a spammer. Which would you rather hear about yourself?

"That Joe Bloggs guy seems okay, but he's always trying to get me to buy something."

"That Joe Bloggs guy really knows what he's talking about. You should read his stuff – you'd pay a fortune to get that kind of advice anywhere else!"

I know which kind of feedback I'd prefer to get.

There are many ways that you can help people though; it doesn't have to be about your particular area of expertise. Perhaps you can introduce somebody to a contact of yours that they've been hoping to meet or recommend a venue that would be perfect for their first speaking engagement.

Networking is all about developing relationships with others. Be yourself, be genuine and don't ever think that simply getting to know your fellow networkers is a waste of time because people only do business with people they like. Local business groups, communities and complementary services such as sports masseurs and doctors for physiotherapists are great places to begin a referral-based practice.

If you have a larger practice already, get involved with networking at exhibitions, expos and events. It might not immediately strike you as closely related to your practice but the kind of people you want to meet and know already invest in events, expos and workshops as a matter of routine. Take a course from a visiting expert in public speaking, join a seminar in goal-setting or meet up on an adventure holiday with other entrepreneurs somewhere in the freezing Antarctic ...

The trick is to start thinking more laterally about how you can expand your life, rather than just your practice. Your growth, developing ethos and life experience will automatically benefit your practice almost as a by-product of your having so much fun! The people you meet and with whom you choose to spend your time will impact your life in every positive way, personally and professionally.

If it's true that 'you are the average of the five people with whom you spend the majority of your time', then make sure that you spend yours with people who inspire you. This is the best way to spread the word about how great your practice is and to build your brand.

BUILDING YOUR BRAND

This is more to do with personality than business. Your brand is all about you – not your practice. You are your brand: your practice will be influenced by your brand whether it's good or bad.

Advertisers will tell you that building a brand is more of a 'touchy-feely' exercise than developing a one off, tactical campaign that aims to sell a product or service. Branding advertising does not necessarily carry a call to action or seek a measurable response from a target market. It is, however, a very valuable part of the marketing process for any business. Just ask Nike, McDonald's, Disneyworld or any of the others that spend a fortune on their branding every year.

Having said that, none of these companies invests their advertising budget in branding alone. Alongside this strategic form of advertising, they will run a tactical, 'response driven' campaign when they need it – an offer or a sale of some kind. Without the branding going on all the time in the background, though, the results of the response-driven campaign would suffer. Why? Because the branding campaign keeps the company top of mind, always visible and perceivably 'bigger' than their competitors who are not advertising with a branding presence.

You don't need knee-buckling amounts of cash to throw at your own branding campaigns though. Create on-line content. Videos and blogs are a great way to increase your online visibility; a short video on your specialty can show that you're a thought leader or innovator in your field. Keep providing that 'top of mind awareness' and when you're ready to sell something, your market will be open to investing in your product or service rather than your closest competitor's, as long as they are looking for what you have to offer.

EPILOGUE

Long ago, in Chapter 4, we looked at Visualisation and what a fabulous tool it can be for affecting your future and realising your dreams. I mentioned that the other three tools you can use to change the way you view your circumstances and to start respecting yourself (as you cannot respect everyone else if you don't respect yourself first) are Gratitude, Goodwill and Compassion.

GET GRATEFUL

Everybody seems to talk about this these days. You've heard it so often you're rolling your eyes. But studies have shown that if you feel genuinely grateful for what is manifested around you, your life will be longer, happier and healthier. So before you skim to the end of this section, take a moment and answer the next question:

Do you give a damn?

Because if you do, you need to understand the power of feeling thankful. As though your cup is overflowing already. As though your dreams are already being realised as you read this. Without that understanding of how far you've come, how much help you've had along the way, how far you can take this baby, you're not going to progress further.

If you don't give a damn, you've just spent hours reading a book that you refuse to let give you the kick up the backside you're secretly seeking. Am I right?

It's time to give up your 'drama' and look at your life realistically.

Few people truly feel grateful. We're prone to take good things for granted. This 'spoilt brat' syndrome has been acknowledged for so long that it actually has an academic title: "Hedonic Adaptation". We simply assume that we're owed good things by virtue of the hard work or time that we put in to attain them. Were you to ask anybody who's lived through warfare or a personal crisis, though, they'd tell you that you don't always reap what you sow. Sometimes, Life just deals you a rotten hand.

Have another look at the cards you're holding right now. Which card should you save? Which should you get rid of at the earliest opportunity? Which ought you hang on to that might just work in your favour?

If you can harness the power of 'gratitude', you can see those cards objectively. Take a positive step forward to achieving the results you want. If you can't feel grateful for this ephemeral stuff right now, that's fine. Perhaps it does sound a bit Enid Blytonish. But it's true that the more you focus on the good stuff, the more of it you'll receive.

So here's something you can do to get yourself in a grateful mood.

Write an account in the third person about yourself; that is to say, if a news reporter were writing a piece on your life, what would they say?

"Ross leads an adventurous life. When he's not meeting new colleagues and visiting places he never learned about in his school geography lessons, he's hanging out with his favourite people and loving family life. He works with colleagues of his choice and is loved and respected by them in return. He gets to work on projects that he's passionate about and has begun to see differences that his time and energy have made in people's lives. What's more, he has a car that starts when he wants it to."

Now, do that for yourself. Write in the third person and look for the great headlines. Go for it for at least fifteen minutes without stopping – and then save the document. This is a piece of work that you can call on in the future, every time you're feeling flat.

GOODWILL AND COMPASSION

It's a prerequisite for anyone in our profession to have both, of course. But what's the betting you've had days when your patience has worn thin! When the pressure is on and you're feeling short on time and empathy, it can be hard to access those reserves of goodwill and compassion that make you a star healthcare practitioner.

Visualisation exercises can help you to lift yourself out of a dour state and refocus on your patient's needs. Use your new tool of relaxation and visualisation to hone in on your patient's feelings for the time that you spend with them. Ask yourself:

- What would it have been like for them growing up? The years they spent at school, studying or working since then?
- What is it like for them now – today, in their present circumstances both at work and at home?
- How would they be feeling right now if they had only a short time to live? What would they want to achieve? Who would they want to hug and why?

Compassion is at the heart of everything we do as health practitioners. If you're not 'feeling it' right now, the onus is on you to change your psychological state and make sure that you do. It's neither impossible nor something that's left to chance: you can choose to feel compassionate or empathic right now.

HAVE FUN!

I recommend that you make this a core value in itself. As we spend a third of our lives at work, it seems a shame not to enjoy it. If you're not having fun at work, you should start looking for ways to change that.

Traditional wisdom states that "Work is not supposed to be fun" and there is this idea that if someone is having fun at work they must be slacking off. The thing that I always hated when I was working for somebody else's clinic was having to 'look busy' whenever the boss was around. This entire notion makes no sense. I would rather see people having fun at work whilst getting their work done at the same time!

Humour in the workplace has the following benefits:

- Improved morale
- Increased productivity
- Improved employee satisfaction and loyalty.
- Increased creativity and innovation

Right now, you might be thinking, "I'd love to do these things at work, but I'm not the boss of my own practice yet!" If that's the situation that you're in, arm yourself with all the evidence that's out there that proves that having fun at work makes employees more productive and more creative. Create a list of some of the things that you and your team could introduce to the practice to lift the mood and present it in your next meeting with your line manager. You never know – you might change the mood in the place for everybody more quickly than you imagine. Later, when you're ready to launch your own practice, you'll know from the start how to make it a place where top practitioners want to work.

If you're considering going into private practice or you've already started your own, I hope you've found this book encouraging and helpful. Over the years in private practice I haven't met many clinicians with an abundance of spare time on their hands. I remember working from the minute the alarm went off every morning until the minute my head touched the pillow at night. It was non-stop and of course it wasn't all about treating patients: I was answering all the phone calls, emails, scheduling and rescheduling appointments, sending invoices and chasing invoices, finding the right accountant, trialling different software, scouring the internet for various pieces of information ... the list went on.

Of course, this was all on top of my being a husband, a dad, a friend and someone with his own hobbies and interests as well. It dawned on me that I wasn't a physio anymore but a salesman, an office manager, a bookkeeper, a marketing expert and an admin expert who still had time to hoover the clinic room on a weekend to keep it looking patient-ready.

What could I do to get off this treadmill without jeopardising all I had worked so hard for?

The answer was startlingly simple - but that didn't make it easily achievable. I could see clearly that by delegating these other tasks I could free up hours and hours of time each week; I'd be able to treat more patients, be a more present husband and father, get in a few extra rounds of fair-weather golfing.

The turn off for me was that delegating these tasks would have cost money. Sure, I would have benefited enormously from hiring my own secretary or office manager – my clinic was already busy - but I couldn't quite justify the expenditure.

It took a few hard lessons, home truths and very supportive family and close social circle to see me through those early years of learning to stand on my own two feet. Learning to take a chance on a calculated risk here and there, moving forward when I really didn't feel like it, accepting responsibility for the things that went wrong ... it's been a roller coaster but well worth the ride.

I hope that now that you've read more about my journey, your own will become a little less pressured as you are able to make better decisions faster for your practice.

You are not alone; if you need more ideas on how to move forward in your brave new career, visit our website www.the-ahg.com and Facebook group www.facebook.com and search: 'Advanced Health Group' for more resources – and while you're there, drop us a line and say 'hi'.

Good luck, and remember: Respect Everyone, Be Memorable, Be Positive and Be the Best version of you that you can be.

Ross

In addition to thanking Joanne my wife, I would like to thank Jo Collie from Imaginantics and Clare McCabe from Purple Star Design for helping make this book a reality.

BIBLIOGRAPHY

Adesso, P. J "Management Would Be Easy if it Weren't For The People" *AMACOM*

Ashton, R "How To Be a Social Entrepreneur, Make Money& Change the World" *CAPSTONE 2010*

Carnegie, D "How To Win Friends and Influence People"

Cornish, S and Tucker, H "Build a Business from Your Kitchen Table" *SIMON & SCHUSTER 1997*

Evans, P "Controlling People" *ADAMS MEDIA*

Henry, T "The Accidental Creative" *PENGUIN 2011*

Hoffman, R and Casnocha, B "The Start-Up of You" *PENGUIN 2013*

Turner, C "The Eureka Principle" *ELEMENT*

Witt, C "Real Leaders Don't Do Powerpoint: How to Speak So People Listen" *PIATKUS 2009*

Rock, D "Your Brain At Work" NEW YORK: *HARPERBUSINESS, 2009*

MORE PRAISE FOR THE BUSINESS OF HEALTH

Ross gives lots of examples which illustrate his ideas perfectly. In addition to this, within each chapter he suggests actionable steps which will improve your being, your thinking and your doing. I read this book after a tough, tiring week, and it was just the tonic to encourage me to check in with myself, implement the content into my life and my business, and remind myself how privileged we are to live in an age where so much potential can be realised. Thank you Ross,! I will be going back for many more sittings and using your book for healthy snacking for months and years to come.

Marcus Nelson, The Mind & Body Coach

There are so many business and self-improvement books out there that as a small business owner it is daunting to know in which direction to look. In his book, Ross has managed to concisely pull together the knowledge he has gleaned throughout his journey from employee to successful business owner. The result is an extremely useful starting point for any employee, manager, business owner or budding entrepreneur, not just in the health-care setting, who wants to gain a better understanding of how to improve their business, and more importantly, their lives. By reading this book, you will discover where your natural strengths and weaknesses lie and what areas you can improve on. On top of this, the top tips Ross gives will help you to begin that journey to improvement to be the best version of you.

Juliet Raine. Physiotherapist and Ergonomic Consultant at EPF Limited

If you want to read a book about clinical skills, this may not be the one for you. However, if you want to read a book about building you own practice you may have picked the right one. In "The Business of Health" Ross Tomkins aims to fill in the gap in the knowledge base of physiotherapy practitioners that have already been exploring the private sector, or wish to venture in setting up their own practice. The book focuses on four qualities/values; respect, being memorable, positive and the best one can be. These qualities are delved into to produce a practical guide and help practitioners build a successful practice avoiding many pitfalls that they may encounter in the process. It is clear that these values reflect Ross's approach to his business and approach to general life. This book is more than a "recipe" for a success, but also an open deep and honest reflection onto Ross's own experiences of clinical, business and personal life outlining the lessons he has learned, the mistakes he has made and the battles that he has won. These experiences are easily relatable for someone who has worked in the private sector and promote one to take risks that may be scared to take. An unintended outcome of this book is that it does benefit one's clinical skills when it comes to communication, critical for any individual; clinician or not, working in public or private sector, involved in healthcare or not. Overall this is a great easy read guide for individuals that wish to explore the rough terrain of working in the corporate healthcare environment.

Georgios Christopoulos. Senior Physiotherapist

This book represents the common sense values and forward thinking perspective of a physio or health care professional in building their practice. The sections highlight and reflect the importance and the variance of communication available to us as therapists, whether that be with clients or colleagues in the work place. Hard work, passion, and drive are all essential traits required to succeed in business and shine through in Ross's early journey but all work and no play doesn't make for a happy or sustainable existence and the book clearly demonstrates the requirement for delegation and the need for colleagues with the same ethos within your practice to develop and be successful. An inspirational read to those starting their journey in business and a reflective read with poignant reminders and values to those already established. A must read.

Will Dykes. Director Hadleigh Physiotherapy Ltd